D1556636

Keith Shackleton

Keith Shackleton

AN AUTOBIOGRAPHY IN PAINTINGS

SWAN·HILL
PRESS

This book is dedicated with gratitude,
to all those who have encouraged me over
the years – by their enjoyment of
my work.

First published in the UK in 1998
by Swan Hill Press, an imprint of Airlife Publishing Ltd

British Library Cataloguing-in-Publication Data
A catalogue record for this book
is available from the British Library

ISBN 1 84037 014 9

Typeset by Servis Filmsetting Ltd.
Printed in Italy

Swan Hill Press
an imprint of Airlife Publishing Ltd
101 Longden Road, Shrewsbury, SY3 9EB, England

Acknowledgements

Because the pictures reproduced in this book come from across the world, gratitude is widespread – and for all kinds of reasons.

Some are easier to acknowledge than others. The distinction for instance, between organisations and those acting on their behalf, become confused. I can only hope that within the corporate name, those individuals will recognise themselves, remember our association and accept my thanks for all it has meant to me.

Here is a list of the organisations whose pictures are featured; who have not only done me the honour of aquiring my work in the first place, but extended continuing kindness and friendship in the years that followed: British Steel, British Aircraft Corporation, Group 4, The Leigh Yawkey Woodson Art Museum – Winconsin, Mill Pond Press – Florida, The Morrison Construction Group, The Peoples Trust for Endangered Species, The Royal Marines, The Royal National Lifeboat Institution, The Royal Society for the Protection of Birds, Royle Publications, Shell UK, Solomon & Whitehead, Swedish Match, The Tryon & Swann Gallery, Uganda National Parks.

Private patrons have made their own varied contributions, by the loan of their pictures, by arranging for photography and by providing information about dates and dimensions to complete the record. Here gratitude goes hand-in-hand with an apology. Had I been a more organised sort of person and kept proper records myself, they could have been spared much of this upheaval. Though some have endured more than others my thanks go to them all.

They include: George Blunt, Peter and Janet Burnell, Ron and Kathleen Cole, Patricia Collins, Neil Cooper, Roger Croson, Tony Foster Andrew and Julia Green, Dr Robin Griffiths, Wink and Muriel Hartranft, Dorothy, David and Robin Hosking, David Houston, Capt. Peter Krasinski, Sir John and Lady Lea, Dr John Levinson, Dr Lyall Watson, Brigadier Peter Madsen, Sheila McCullagh, Dr Lois Myers, Julian Royle, Sarah, Jason and Jasper Shackleton, Charles Whitehead, Sir Max Williams.

Particular mention must be made of Peter and Carole Holland and of Oliver Swann. Between them they have offered not only their pictures but every kind of help, advice and support from the beginning, as well as proving irresistibly persuasive in their convention that nothing is impossible – once you make a start.

In making that start, Clare Pawley proved a tower of strength by her resourcefulness in photographing a great many pictures held in store, under far from ideal conditions.

Through Alastair Simpson and Swan Hill Press came the whole idea of this book, to emerge in symbiotic relationship with my wife Jacq's plans for a Retrospective Exhibition at the Mall Galleries in London, in March 1998. The encouragement, confidence and wisdom of the whole staff of Swan Hill Press, has been constant and invaluable.

Finally there is Jacq herself. A eulogy of some kind, about the part played by authors' ever-loving/long-suffering spouses, under 'Acknowledgements,' is almost an article of mandatory protocol – thereby risking perhaps, the loss of a little conviction! But I know *now* that wives exist who actually carry the work along, forsaking their own many interests for as long as it takes to put everything into the publisher's hands.

My thanks go to Jacq not so much for being patient and 'helpful' but for a great deal more.

Keith Shackleton
Woodleigh, Devon

Contents

Seventy-five – a Preamble

Suddenly I am seventy-five years old. This must be so because it is 1998 as I write and I was born in 1923.

'Four score years less five' and 'three quarters of a century' are poetic alternatives suggested to emphasise the significance of all this but nothing can disguise the fact that as statistics go, it is hardly worth a candle. Most people get there and the numbers are increasing. Moreover, when they do, most of them see little need to make a big deal out of it.

Though I have never given it a thought until now – my wife has. She announced her resolve, in a very heart-warming way and with the connivance of friends, to arrange a Retrospective Exhibition at the Mall Galleries in London of as many of my pictures as could be brought together, to mark the event.

'It has nothing to do with you,' she said. '*I* shall do it. It will be a good excuse for a party. You go back to the studio and play . . . .' But this book grew directly from her plans and suddenly 'playing in the studio' had to be a lot more constructive than usual.

When things like this happen they do at least concentrate the mind. A mental stock-taking is called for – and some personal retrospect. I am having to admit to myself that I have reached 'codgerhood.' I must now set down a few significant events because they are needed not only for the exhibition but for this text as well.

To begin with, I am currently and without shame, enjoying my second childhood. The first was fun too all those years ago and it hummed along like a well-oiled bicycle for a whole lifetime, moving inexorably as glaciers move, towards this second one. Most people I suspect, enjoy a period of quite lengthy and sober adulthood after reaching maturity before the eccentricities of dotage begin to move in. For me, actual childhood and second childhood were one, without so much as a hiccup in between – four-score-years-less-five of it. The same things delight me now that delighted me when I was six. It is just that though little moss may have been gathered along the way, I have learned a lot more about the stone – and where it rolled.

Drawing and painting were present at the very beginning – in the genes. My father was a pioneer aeroplane designer with a great eye for shape. My mother executed the loveliest abstract doodles on her telephone pad, shading them into exciting relief and meaningful forms, then over a later call adding cast shadows that seemed to lift them from the paper. So there were always crayons, chalks, drawing blocks and assorted pencils in Christmas stockings with limitless encouragement and constructive criticism to go with them.

Later these Christmas gifts were to compete with fishing tackle, shrimping nets and the like but by then I had graduated to water-paints and even an easel of sorts. Parallel distractions on the seashore or along the river bank actually enhanced the enthusiasm for drawing rather than overwhelming it. Drawing things that interested me was always a sort of homage. In a way it was my personal statement of gratitude for the experience. Yet my parents, despite being unflinchingly supportive, had both been indoctrinated with the prevalent misconception of the day that all artists were destined to die penniless and starving in garrets. Prospects of prosperity in the profession were simply nil.

I fear none of this early work is here because none has survived. Much was kept in the family for a year or two then cleared away in a move of house or even country. Five years and early schooling in Australia had been a productive period for me but I was always my own hardest taskmaster, always felt that the *next* work would be the one worth keeping. If I finished anything that halfway pleased me I generally gave it away to friends and enjoyed in return a grateful and encouraging little pat on the head.

In the early thirties we were back in England and I went to boarding school at Oundle, to encounter for the first time, a proper art master. By the time I left school, well into the War, I had studied under two more and learned something different from each.

They were a wonderfully rakish lot. None could have been mistaken for anything but 'artists' yet their flexibility and genius enabled them to harmonise with a background of conventional school discipline. By far their most important contribution to my personal artistic contentment was to introduce me to oil paints – one of my life's first great longings. Like most children I had been raised on watercolours and like most children found them inordinately difficult, which led to frustration and finally to a state of total discouragement.

I had looked longingly at the family oil portraits that hung in my grandfather's, my great uncle's and my great aunt's houses. The thick, juicy, richness of the paint was a real siren. It stood out a mile to me that here was a medium I could get hold of and force it to obey me, instead of one that served up something I had never intended and certainly did not want.

Of all the portraits, one hanging in my great aunt's house in Folkestone was paramount in my affections – *Redcoat*. He had been an Admiral in Nelson's Navy I was told – a wonderfully bucolic-looking fellow with a twinkle in the eye and clearly a robust intake of grog had gone into his complexion. He was seated, with a silver-topped cane in his hand and gazed impassively out of his frame while a horrendous battle raged behind him and smoke drifted across the stricken French fleet beyond.

However, it was the treatment of the folds in the red coat and the gold braid that grabbed me. The paint was so thick it was like bas-relief. This was for me. I could see the medium that had put such power into *Redcoat* transferred to the subject matter of wild animals

and wild places which were then, as they are now, my all-time favourites. My ambition to paint in oils was soon to be fulfilled.

I suspect that in the thirties art education was much the same in all schools. There was a general understanding that drawing was important. Unless one could reasonably delineate a shape, interpret perspective and understand about the relative scale of objects, any attempt to jump the gun and get straight into advanced painting became a sterile, ungrounded exercise. The 'progressive' notion that any form of craftsmanship, any recognisable skill with pencil or brush was retrograde, had yet to be invented.

Our teachers, however bohemian in dress and demeanour believed that while making a mess could certainly be fun, an altogether better mess was possible if one knew how to draw it first.

Drawing periods consisted of just one hour per week. Whole classes attended and they were held in the official Art Room. The paraphernalia of conventional art teaching lay around – cubes and cones, plaster busts and classic figures, orderly stacks of drawing boards, easels and 'donkeys.' I remember the parquet floor, the high Gothic windows, the piles of sugar-paper and the all-pervading smell of beeswax and poster paints. The Art Room was a very clinical place, its order and cleanliness ensured by Mr Plowright the custodian, who cycled in each morning with superb dignity from his home at Warmington, five miles away, to order the smooth running of his domain.

My first art teacher was Richard Finney and it was he who introduced me without delay to an entirely different field of human activity available in the school – Voluntary Studio!

Voluntary Studio had nothing whatsoever to do with the Art Room beyond the fact that the art teacher of the day presided over both and it was, of course, voluntary. Studio happened on Tuesday and Thursday evenings each week, from five until seven. We drew, painted,

sculpted or printed whatever and how we wantcd, but guidance was always to hand and encouragement aplenty. Compared to the Art Room, it was a classic example of one volunteer being worth ten conscripts. Moreover, because it was miles from the centre of things and located in a decrepit and deconsecrated tin chapel, the whole ambience of the place was in tune with the informal, off-the-hook atmosphere that prevailed. It was under such fertile conditions that my introduction to oils began.

Richard Finney was a perfectionist and insisted on a set lesson to launch his *ab-initio* painters. He had chosen a stuffed owl for a model, which I found very acceptable, and three of us would-be Rembrandts were kept at this owl for the best part of a term. At last the attentive Finney must have noted that morale was cracking and announced, 'OK boys. Forget the owl. Paint whatever you like!'

This was my moment. Before the Studio was locked up that evening I had come up with a leaping salmon – my first entirely free painting in oils, straight out of my head. It was a messy little work but nevertheless a milestone. The door had opened and I had felt the hedony of this rewarding medium. Linseed oil and turpentine were to remain a major background of my life until the very present and, I hope, well into the future.

Richard Finney left to join an artists' group in Cornwall and was replaced by Guy Burn who was left-handed and had a very pretty French wife. It was he who added yet another dimension to Voluntary Studio by instigating the 'Sketch Club'. This took us into the countryside on Saturday afternoons, on hired bicycles of low mechanical integrity, or if we were lucky, in Guy Burn's ancient Aston Martin. 'Fi-Fi' Burn often came too. ('I loff painting zee naked trees.')

We painted barns, river scenes and lots of naked trees and I discovered the unexpected propensity of oils to attract insects which would wade knee-deep through a rendering of blue sky and clouds often imparting, quite unwittingly, a little extra 'patina' to the quality of the paint.

One day I made another discovery based on the slow-drying properties of the medium. I had painted two small pictures during the afternoon – different views of the same barn-yard and both horrible enough to be wiped clean. On an inpulse of disgust, however, I slammed them together, face-to-face and for good measure, rotated them through about fifteen degrees. They came apart with the noise nowadays associated with Velcro to reveal two thoroughly exciting and brilliantly-executed little works. 'Fi-Fi was enchanted by their sensitivity and insisted on buying one on the spot – my very first picture sale. I had discovered the magic of the 'happy accident' in painting. I had discovered too that such phenomena constituted a further bonus for oils. Any accidents in water-colours had always been *un*happy ones.

Guy Burn was succeeded in time by Pat Millard, a man of enormous character and full of surprises. He had been involved in the Spanish Civil War, was deeply concerned with ceramic design and much in demand as a stand-in cricket coach. A few artists, in my experience, were also demon bowlers and batsmen with the eye of a weasel. Later, by coincidence and after the War was over, he taught my wife Jacq as head of the Regent Street Polytechnic School of Art. His memory is evergreen between us for she still passes on to me little scraps of advice she learned from him. Because of the war I had missed any chance of an art school proper and ironically enough, learned little gems of what they had to offer via my old teacher – by proxy.

Being ridiculously young at the time, the Second World War was something that I played by ear and made what I could of events as they unfolded. A more mature mind would have been occupied with the stupidity, the waste, the sheer horror of it all. At least all of us, young or old, accepted first the inevitability of

it and secondly the conviction that at all costs, it must be won. Its only saving grace was that such unification of purpose produced a feeling of comradeship in the land which has never been seen since – until it surfaced again unexpectedly, at the funeral of Princess Diana.

From a painting point of view there were certain opportunities and I was able to take them as they came. I found myself posted into a section of the RAF that dealt with camouflage and there were several very fine painters in this group. I began to understand how it was that artists' 'groups' can stimulate the best work from individual members because they are mutually supportive. Inspiration is infectious.

I could understand how Richard Finney had been so enthusiastic about his group in Newlyn. I learned much from my fellow 'erks' and it all helped to pass the time.

However, camouflage by its very nature, is concerned with protection – it is largely defensive. When the tide turned and the War

took on a more aggressive mien, our little section began to stagnate. I sought through the Air Ministry Department of Public Relations, something of a roving commission – simply to go out and paint the War.

Those last years were stimulating in many ways. I learned for instance, what can be achieved in official circles with the combination of a rubber-stamped pass from Whitehall and an air of assurance – even without a clip-board to add conviction.

I found myself on patrol in the Channel with RN Coastal Forces and formed a deep affection for the motor torpedo boats and the splendid scenes they provided by night – the criss-cross of red and green tracer and the hanging star-shells that made artificial moon-paths across the sea.

The War ended in Europe soon after and at a moment when I was actually overlooking Dunkirk from an artillery observation post and heard Churchill's message on a headset. Dunkirk was in fact the last German resistance in Europe. Soon after, I went on to the Far East but paintings of this fairly turbulent period mostly went their separate ways.

It was required that drawings and pictures had to be sent in for 'censorship' – I suppose a necessary precaution. Later I would learn that some sensitive piece of equipment had been featured and the work therefore impounded. I never seemed to mind or make much effort to get them back. The pleasure they had afforded in their making, was passed. The most decisive loss was when a whole winter's work was destroyed with MTB 776 in Ostend Harbour – but the loss of human life and the loss of a few sketches stood no comparison.

The pattern of the War was a day-to-day affair for everyone. I had learned few lessons of husbandry or thought much about the future. I painted pictures that I gave to my friends – by-passing the censor who already had the lion's share – and that period ended for me with little of an artistic nature to show for it. I had however survived. I was a civilian again, and a grateful nation gave me a little brown suit and a trilby.

On 29 July 1942 my elder brother Allen was lost. He was posted 'missing believed killed in action' when his Spitfire failed to return with one other, after an operational sweep over Belgium. Three weeks later would have been his twenty-first birthday.

Though it had never been discussed in the family, it was always assumed that Allen would go into our father's business of aircraft design and brokerage when it started up again. Aeroplanes had always been his guiding passion. To me they were just another of life's manifold interests in competition with others. For all that, circumstances had now dictated that I must involve myself more fully in this direction if only for the sake of the family and this was exactly what happened.

Amongst a wealth of unforgettable sayings, my mother had a ninth beatitude, 'Blessed are they that expecteth nothing for they shall not be disappointed.' It is a good working

philosophy. It would be untrue to suggest that I expected *nothing* from my subsequent fifteen years in aviation, but neither was I disappointed. Expectations may have been tarnished by the thought that all this was taking me away from painting, which would have been my first choice – even under the spectre

of starvation in a garret. As it happened, I greatly enjoyed the varied flying, the travel it offered and the lovely people I met. When I finally pulled out it was the people I missed the most. On clear days of sunshine and drifting cumulus I missed the flying too.

The doom-laden predictions of penury levelled at an artistic livelihood were, I suppose, alleviated by the aviation but I still felt determined to work at it whenever I could. Every spare moment was taken up either painting for art society exhibitions or working on commissions of every kind, from book-jackets, calendars and advertising material to

portraits and presentation paintings.

Left to my own devices, however, I painted birds as a first choice – birds and bird places, the sea, the sky, the mountains and the mudflats. Here I must pay tribute to Peter Scott who was one of the very first to break the tradition of bird portraiture and paint them as the living part of their landscape. The flood gates are now open and we are all the richer for it. For me, there is no denying his influence especially as it came in the formative years of Oundle's Voluntary Studio. He had known these rewarding evenings fifteen years before me and had been taught in the same place by the forerunners of Finney, Burn and Millard. The coincidence of the situation often struck me when I became one of a new generation of eager schoolboys, all vying with one another to produce their own versions of ducks in flight against a rosy-fingered dawn. The ghosts will be homeless now – alas, the old tin chapel is no more.

My aviation days came to an end when the firm was taken over. By then the fun had gone out of it anyway and it was time to move on. But I soon found that something other than painting was essential if zest was to be preserved in the everyday pattern of life.

I could not paint full-time without losing interest. There had to be another pursuit to take me away so that a return to the studio was a stimulus in itself and the resumption of painting a happy release. The answer of the moment proved to be children's television in the form of the BBC programme *Animal Magic* with Johnny Morris. In some respects it was a sort of busman's holiday, because I was called upon to draw wild animals in the studio as my contribution to the programme as well as trying to pay some heed to the script. With Johnny Morris loose on the set, the problem was to have stopped laughing before the red light flashed on the recording camera.

Involvement with *Animal Magic* lasted about four years and was immediately followed by the realisation of a dream that had persisted since childhood. My ambition was to sail to the Antarctic and may well have had its origins in a distant relative enormously admired, Sir Ernest Shackleton. The means and the occasion was the brand-new ice-working ship *Lindblad Explorer* on her maiden voyage from Southampton in 1969 and I had been taken on as 'naturalist' and boatman.

This versatile little vessel became my home from home for years to come and under her revised name of MV *Explorer* I still keep in touch. A book about her extraordinary global wanderings and sojourns in the Arctic and Antarctic ice was published in 1986. *Ship in the Wilderness* is long since out of print but to me the influence of the ship herself lingers on in many of the pictures in *this* book; their origins were aboard her and in the exciting areas where she sailed.

Seventy-five years is a long time to condense into a few paragraphs. There was a call for some sort of biographical note to set a time scale against the pictures and the influences of the day that lurked behind each one. Somehow this became *auto*biographical. When I started putting recollections together, I came under pressure to carry on and write it myself. Times and dates and places are one thing, memories are another. They are acutely personal, like the

subtle and seductive blend of elation, misgiving and downright grief that attends the painting of most pictures.

So to fill the purpose of these notes, I must mention certain important events and dates as a framework and allow the rest to emerge with comments relating to each separate picture where it appears.

I was born in Weybridge, Surrey, then a delightful, rural village in which my grandfather was the local doctor and counted among his patients several gipsy families who lived in horse-drawn, painted caravans. Another patient was the blacksmith who shod the shirehorses that towed narrowboats on the Basingstoke Canal. All the river meadows in summer seemed to hold a corncrake and every pond held frogs, toads, newts and sticklebacks. My grandfather was one of that breed of encyclopedic naturalists that every country boy craves for a companion. We shortly moved to Scotland and later to Melbourne, Australia and we all missed him and his influence. He died in 1933.

With the War behind us and the general feeling of euphoria that followed, any spare time was taken up racing the International 14′ dinghies in summer and exploring tidal creeks in winter in search of wild geese – with a punt. Later on I will try to explain something that is often hard to understand, but which in the interests of truth, has to be mentioned.

Through sailing I met my wife Jacq and we married in September 1951. In 1953 our daughter was born and though christened Sarah, has been known as 'Sook' to everyone since her birth. Jason followed in 1955 (at that

'..... and into the Beaufort Sea.'

time we knew only two other Jasons and one was a black labrador). Our third child, Jasper, arrived in 1957 and like his sister, soon acquired a popular soubriquet – he is universally known as 'Spin.' There are now eight grandchildren at large and I have heard the situation compared with *Watership Down*.

The genes I mentioned earlier, both Jacq's and mine, carry on revealing themselves in their separate ways. Though none of our children would actually put a canvas on an easel and paint a picture, I have a feeling that one day they will. In the meantime, other outlets of enormous vigour take its place.

Sarah is a fashion designer but with an infectious enthusiasm for other pursuits – jewellery-making and design, wood-turning, sculpture, basket-making and more recently, a local life-class in which Jacq also takes part. She and her family live close by and we see them often.

Jason in his early childhood, gave every indication of finding himself, one day, in the starvation-in-a-garret business. He used to watch me paint for long periods in an unnerving, rapt silence. When I had gone out, he would take up the paint-laden brushes from the jar on the table, and with wild, expressive strokes embellish the foreground (he could reach no higher) of the picture in hand. He particularly enjoyed working on seascapes because a little of the wild abandon he liked was already in place.

There were times when the Muse was so active he continued his brush strokes over the walls, or took to the fingers as I often do, massaging the paint with eager, starfish hands into the canvas, the curtains, the furniture before – ever the tidy boy – wiping them clean on his T-shirt. For the first time I began to understand why harassed mothers preferred their young to be watercolourists.

Some of these pictures seemed to have acquired a new and exciting dimension – and were signed with Jason's handiwork inviolate. Most things can be done in differing ways and

nothing comes healthier than co-operation – even with a boy of three.

He is now a potter of renown and to my mind, enormous talent. His skills run to tile-hung murals and commemorative ceramics of striking size and diversity, as well as the most delicate jewellery. He and his wife Jessica and their two 'wee girls' live in the loveliest part of Dumfries and Galloway.

Jasper, our youngest, designs and builds furniture (and boats) and we shall hear more of him later. He has a son, Max. One day when Max was about five years old, he came into the studio and stood watching, just as his Uncle Jason had done, silent and enthralled by the application of paint. I thought to myself, with mounting unease – here we go again!

Instead he spoke, and asked a question that is not as easy to answer as it might seem:

'Keiff?'

'Yes Max,'

'Keiff. Do you ever get pissed-off with painting?'

In 1974 my father died, just a year short of eighty and the following year, my mother. She was very special to us all and is remembered not just by a host of immortal sayings but by shrubs and trees growing here in Devon, from cuttings she had struck for us years ago in her garden beside Chichester Harbour.

I have sometimes wondered what my parents would have made of their prediction for an artist's destiny, had they been alive today. There has been no starvation, no garrets, for any of my painting friends – nor for me. However, they never could have foreseen what a fertile and encouraging climate was awaiting artists in the last quarter of the twentieth century. Certainly I have no regrets about embarking on an artistic career, even though I am sure the elite of the 'Art' scene would dismiss my efforts as 'decadent'– at best.

Contemplation of the future is nothing if not enjoyable to the optimist. These past few years

have taught me that paint-brushes, as tools of a creative trade, have many competitors. The scythe, the spade, the chainsaw and the brushcutter are all means to a very fulfilling end but are concerned with a canvas measured in acres.

Home is now a nature reserve and I am busy on what will have to be the final ambition – to recreate a little piece of country the like of which could be found anywhere in England, even up to the very outskirts of London, 75 years ago.

Zavodovski –
Mt. Asphyxia – bearing 240°

M.V. 'LINDBLAD EXPLORER'   South Sandwich Islands.

The Puntgunner

Oil on canvas 20″ x 24″ (1941)

I had misgivings about including this picture and not just on artistic grounds. Seeing it again today it brings an echo of another life that might well have belonged to somebody else.

It represents a specific and rather dedicated period – long ago. Since the picture surfaced unexpectedly in a sale room and was bought by an old friend, the event seemed more like a behest to include it than a simple coincidence.

Now it is here, I feel no need whatever for contrition. Because attitudes can change so abruptly in a lifetime, it is interesting to consider the thoughts that were there when it all happened and less than honest to deny they ever existed.

My parents, their friends and my own friends and relations were all predominately country people – as their forebears had been. In consequence my brother and I were brought up to accept and respect firearms and to shoot straight in the same way as we were taught to ride bicycles and ponies, to use a scythe and a cross-cut saw and the importance of shutting gates. Parallel with this came a total involvement with boats which as a background to life has outlasted them all.

There is nothing like success to motivate children. I began to get good scores on targets and win prizes, and became involved in rifle-shooting as much as with the gun. I was passionately fond of stalking because it put another dimension of purpose into a day on the hill. It had nothing whatever to do with being a blood-thirsty little creep. For the same reason I was drawn into wildfowling, and puntgunning in particular, for that meant getting afloat.

People talk darkly of the 'gun culture' and there has been horrifying proof of what a sort of 'gun worship' can do to the minds of psychopaths – but it bears no comparison with the sort of things we got up to when young, or what a large proportion of my friends get up to now.

I say 'my friends' because I am no longer personally involved. The occasional rabbit or brace of wood pigeons in a pie simply states that we are not vegetarians – the 'sport' element equates with a visit to the super-market.

Soon after the War finished, I began to think more for myself rather than the conditioned reflexes of upbringing. It would be easy to say that I had suddenly discovered humanity, but I was always humane. This is the hardest thing to explain to anyone who has never known the experience.

The truth was, I believe, that I had discovered, along with many others, the incomparable pleasure of leaving wild things undisturbed, of watching their behaviour and retiring in silence with the memory intact. A gunshot became an intrusion and despoiled the calm.

Seeing and leaving alone, however, requires some skill too and I believe this was acquired in my case, through those early days of hunting – ashore and afloat. So I can claim no regrets for the experience. Had I possessed some small ability with a camera, I know just what direction I would have taken.

Confronted with this picture after so many years, I notice funny little things about it. That fashionably stylised over-simplification of the water and the mud shapes are straight from the art input of school days. I was trying so hard to be 'with it.' I was proclaiming that being up to the eyes in mud, soaked to the skin and behaving like a pirate did not prevent me from being a sensitive and highly creative little fellow. Had the term 'trendy' been invented then, I am sure I would have accepted the word as designed for me.

Yet there was one other factor that came through, and that was the reminder of what it felt like out on the shore and creeping up the creeks. Puntgunning was conducted either with a kindred spirit in a double punt, or alone – and more than anything else I have done, combined a total detachment from the world at large with a hands-on involvement with the tidal surroundings and a very elusive quarry which paradoxically, I deeply loved.

Indeed they were wonderful days – but never again . . .

The Stranger from Greenland

Oil on Canvas 20″ x 24″ (1948)

It can be unsettling to read lines you wrote long ago. Views and ideas change and when looked at again after much dust has settled there is always a risk of embarrassment.

This picture, *The Stranger from Greenland*, was painted in the late forties, very soon after the War, and was one of those which I felt at the time, had 'come off.' Later, when my wife and I were married in 1951, I gave it to my new in-laws so that it would stay in the family and so it has. It now belongs to my brother-in-law, Charles Whitehead.

In my first book, *Tidelines*, I had described this picture and some of the thoughts that lay behind it. In subject matter, it was a fair example of what my old art teacher, Pat Millard used to call 'composition' and he delivered the word with a sort of ecclesiastical reverence which filled it with artistic wealth. A composition implied something fanciful, arranged so that the subjects' shapes in their interplay with each other, as well as the sympathetically contrived background, would achieve the elusive quality called 'movement' – the word spoken, likewise, in dramatic tremolo.

Inevitably I read the passage from *Tidelines* again, and found to my surprise that as far as this picture is concerned, the description could as easily have been written last week as fifty years ago.

Since this is an autobiography in pictures, and pictures that are qualified with words, I shall return to the old narrative at the moment when the design was roughed out on the canvas in charcoal – a group of pink-footed geese flying from right to left – but I had apparently reached an impasse over what to do next.

It was weeks later that *The Stranger* occurred to me. The painting, half-drawn, stood with its face to the studio wall where I had left it when other things intervened. When one leaves a picture this way and, as it were, surprises it at a later date, it will always look better or worse than was imagined – never the same. Shutting it off from sight has given time for its whole countenance to slide out of memory, then suddenly confronted with it again one might almost be seeing the work of another. If critical with oneself when put to the wall it may look encouraging on second sight, but, whatever else, if there is a discordant detail in the composition it will cry out for notice, and one cannot understand how it could have been missed before. So it was with this one, and when I looked at it again it seemed at once that the birds were too uniform in size and interest. The picture lacked some strong dominating feature to give it consequence and was incomplete in object like a portrait without eyes.

Then came the thought of a different bird – a stranger – a white one for preference. The obvious choice was a snow goose, white with black pinions, pink bill and mauve paddles. The more I thought of it, the better the idea seemed to be. It would be faithful to life to paint her bigger than the rest, and her plumage would repeat all the colours of the picture as white must always do. In her singleness she would have a regal and romantic air.

In drawing her with a brush on the canvas I thought of the snow goose I had seen in the south of Ireland and the blue goose from Greenland with which she had mated, and the result of the match, two hybrid young that flew with them wherever they went.

They had kept company with whitefronts, for there are no pinkfeet in County Wexford, but the effect she made among them was the same, because she was bigger and the whitest thing in the dark country. I had seen her in every phase of the changing light, coming in from the strand in the early dawn, a white speck among ten thousand grey ones throughout the day and at evening flight, an orphan spark catching the last of the sun when the whole sky trembled with interwoven meshes of geese. But nearer than all to the picture itself was the memory of flying over her and looking down upon her back as she circled, with the rest, the deep green pattern of the marshes.

By putting her in my picture I hoped that the others would be only passengers beside and behind her, their reticence giving her a dominant lordly air like a gull soaring in the trough of a wave. Then the picture was finished, and although it had begun without her she had completed it – and brought with her its name.

18

Sunlight and *Moonlight*

Oil on canvas 24″ x 20″ (1949)

The selection of pictures for a collection like this, must be guided not only by the merit, or otherwise, of artistic content but what can be seen as a representative milestone in a life that has been led astray by certain seductive pursuits other than painting pictures. The importance of this one is simply that it illustrates a period (quite a long period) when summers were spent/misspent rupturing oneself over the gunwales of a small boat in an effort to sail it a little faster than the opposition.

The fact that the period lasted as long as it did testifies to the enormous fun of it all and I would not have missed a moment of it. When its end finally came it was for no other reason than atrophy of the competitive instinct.

The International Fourteens were a fiercely competitive class. They still are, though they have lost the thoroughbred lines and balanced beauty of hull and sailplan of those I remember. It was certainly never a class in which to develop misgivings about competitive thrust. Better by far to transfer to a single-handed class, or one of the more laid back ones where they race without too much fervour and would admit they are simply having a 'jolly.' For me the time came, and not very long ago, when the suppressed beachcomber and lotus-eater broke out. In the hard racing context, an unwholesome version of the been-there-done-that syndrome emerged and serious competition afloat drew to a close – albeit with considerable grace. As with Ratty however, in *Wind in the Willows*, the 'messing about in boats' bit remains evergreen and I am sure, always will.

On a purely historical note, *Sunlight* and *Moonlight* were the two Uffa Fox-designed International Fourteens representing Great Britain in the team races at Montreal in 1949, competing against Canada, the United States and Bermuda. The crews were Charles Currey and Tony Warrilow (*Sunlight*) and Peter Scott and Keith Shackleton (*Moonlight*).

I am happy to relate that we won – the mention being made with a certain trepidation because today it is no longer fashionable to dwell on minor British triumphs. For that matter we won again a few years later in the next series in Bermuda!

The boats in the picture are on a broad, planning reach, skipping over a benign, if disgustingly coloured sea. The front boat is *Sunlight* with *Moonlight* behind but there is no competition here, this was one of those rare and hallowed jollys – a pause for breath in a dedicated arena of cut and thrust and acute physical discomfort.

Scraperboard 8½″ x 8½″ (1953)

The Farmer's Wings

Oil on canvas 20″ x 24″ (1953)

The aeroplane is a Miles M38 Messenger with its characteristic little gathering of fins and rudders and more than any other, it symbolises for me the fun side of my aviation years.

It is true one felt a little closer to God in open aeroplanes in helmet and goggles, Sidcot suits and flying-boots, but the little Messenger with its rather hedonistic, leather-seated cabin, was a true gentleman's aircraft. It could be flown in a tidy suit to a rural function or even, dare I admit, in a dinner-jacket. The Messenger was tweed rather than denim and a great favourite with aeronautical farmers.

Our little family firm sold lots of them, bought them back and sold them again and whenever we had one footloose in the hangar between owners, it would become a firm's hack and used with much more regularity than a car.

When my wife and I were first married it proved a handy little vehicle to fly down to the Isle of Wight on a summer's evening for a swim or to buy a fresh lobster at the Bembridge Aero Club and be back home again before dusk.

Farmers liked them particularly because you could drop them into a fairly small field which turned any reasonably flat piece of pasture into an aerodrome, sometimes with the added refinement of a discarded pair of trousers for a wind-sock.

The sort of destination in the picture was just perfect for a delivery. The customer would send a detailed sketch-map for finding the field or lay out a marker. Sometimes it would be in a far away corner of Britain involving a pleasantly long journey, unhindered by the irksome concentration of driving on the road.

Then there would be the field, the gentle let-down over the hedge, the soft bump on mown grass, the taxi back to the gate into the lane, the switch off and as the prop made its last jump to rest, silence except for the whirring of the gyro instruments running down and a skylark high above.

I knew the farmer would be delighted with his Miles M38 Messenger. My only sadness was that I would have to go home by train.

Winter Afternoon

Oil on canvas 20" x 24" (1953)

One of the many passions in the life of my father-in-law, Commander Teddy Whitehead, was running with the Beagles. It followed that because my own courtship of his step-daughter Jacq was well underway, and she generally accompanied him, I went along too and felt it a price worth paying.

I have never shied from exertion or indeed discomfort, as a means to a desired end, but would never have chosen it for its own sake. I was never the hair-shirt type but Teddy was, he positively exuded the impression of deriving some inner grace from the process. He just loved running, and in the filthiest conditions. He was a loveable exercise freak.

This painting comes straight from those days, the home counties landscape in winter, his favourite beagling country. But it was seen through the eyes of one who, by Teddy's standards, was a bit of a slob, preferring to sit on a fence and draw, rather than run all after-noon over stubble and ploughed and water-logged fields of kale.

I painted the picture for him because it was his very favourite scene, redolent of damp dis-comfort, frenetic exertion, red rose hips gathered for kick-start nourishment as he ran, then at sunset, a ritual feast of tea, boiled eggs and watercress sandwiches made with whole-meal bread.

I love to think that wherever he is now, he is still doing it.

23

Mother and Babe

Oil on canvas 18″ x 14″ (1954)

This is a sketch in oils of Jacq and our first-born, Sarah, who for reasons too complicated to relate, has been known as 'Sook' almost from birth. Here she is at about six months old.

I have two major regrets – one that I have never kept diaries except on 'expeditions', the other that I did so few drawings or paintings of our children and most of these seem to have vanished.

However, I remember one particular portrait of Sarah when aged about eight, lying on a bed of seaweed. On the spur of the moment and inspired, no doubt, by the incoming tide, I drew out her body from the waist down into the form of a sea-bass. A fine specimen of this shapely fish was lying conveniently on a plate in the larder at the time – and provided the perfect reference.

The finished picture was hung in an RSMA Exhibition at the Guildhall Gallery in London, with the rather ingenuous title *Portrait of a young Mermaid reclining on Fucus vesiculous.*

The sale of a picture has always been vital to artists if only to keep their family's ribs apart, so a red spot on this one was an immediate cause for rejoicing. It is only in recent years that the Mermaid has come to mind, with a little sadness at having no knowledge of its present whereabouts.

Climbing through Mist – Snow Geese

Oil on board 48″ x 72″ (1957)

Apart from a huge mural on a prepared dining-room wall in Connemara, this was the biggest picture I have ever painted.

In those days we lived in a house in London, which in practice meant that much of our lives, complete with children and other livestock, was spent on the A3, between Notting Hill and a little rented cottage on Chichester Harbour. In the average year, time was divided about 50/50 between the two.

For me London was a great place to paint. There were no outdoor distractions – the studio and all that went on there was the escape. I could work all day and every day and get things done, in a little private eyrie with a window to the sky, among the chimney-pots and the cooing pigeons.

If I ran out of Cobalt Blue or Titanium White, there was a little art shop on the corner. If I needed to check a detail at the zoo or the Natural History Muscum, I was off and back again with the answer in a flash. I once calculated that I climbed and decended about 1,500 feet in a working day, in pursuit of such errands – the odd cup of coffee, the sudden urge to feed the turtles in the pond at the back or to recover some item I had left in the hallway. I could readily understand how Whymper (artist and first to climb the Matterhorn) once said that London dwellers made the best mountaineers, because they were 'forced to live in those damned tenements!'

The panel for this huge picture, 48″ x 72″ was duly carried up seven flights of stairs by the resident sherpa, to be carried down again in due passage of time, with this picture on its surface.

It was exhibited and bought by an old friend of my parents. It hung for many years in a lovely room high on a hill, overlooking the Clyde. My parents' friend died and there followed a tortuous chain of events which ended many years later when the *Snow Geese* appeared in a saleroom. They were bought at auction by a very great friend, of a younger generation, who sadly, my parents never met.

In common with most of my pictures, I can now see much wrong with it. I can hear Peter Scott's voice saying, 'Nice picture, but the heads are too big you know.' Of course he was right, but there are times when associations and pure sentiment do much to ameliorate simple oversights and errors in drawing. There is also comfort in the thought that people who actually *know* how big a snow goose's head should be are fairly thin on the ground!

Landfall – 'The Needles' Lighthouse

Oil on board 24″ x 36″ (1959)
Reproduced by Solomon & Whitehead 1960

In 1960 this picture was published as a print by Solomon & Whitehead, and a forgotten copy of it suddenly came to light while rummaging through an old plan-press in the studio store-room. I was really glad to have found it.

It must have been 35 years since I had last seen it. Things tend to go into these sort of drawers and there they stay – as often as not until an executor has to make a posthumous inventory of a lifetime's fallout. In the process of my search, however, a lot of other memories were revived and this particular picture had proved to be the catalyst.

I can remember very well painting it – and even some of the other pictures that stood about the studio at the time. The original had been bought by Max Aitken, then working at the *Daily Express* in Fleet Street. He was particularly fond of The Needles Point through its associations and for many years the picture hung in his house, 'The Prospect', at Cowes.

It reminded him, he said, of those aspects of the Battle of Britain that he liked to remember – *our* side of the Channel and the remorseless fight to keep it that way. In symbolism The Needles are as British as the Cliffs of Dover – as a landfall to homecoming mariners (as well as flyers), a heart warming cause for celebration.

Memories aroused by this old print came like the opening of a Pandora's box, each one leading to another and then another. At the very bottom came all the sharply detailed recollections of making the first drawings of which this picture was the final result. I did them on a knee-pad, in the cockpit of a little aeroplane, in the autumn of 1958.

A diaphanous mist lay over the Isle of Wight. As I approached from across Poole Bay, this familiar wall of razor-backed chalk thrust out towards me, resolving itself with progressive clarity. The lighthouse, bright in colour and ordered in shape, triumphantly marked its tip.

It was late in the afternoon with the sun laying shadows of it all onto the sea. The brightness of the foreground ran away into haze and recession until the Wight finally lost itself in a sort of ethereal mystery.

I had the little plane flying at its slowest without stalling, flaps down and throttled back as I drew in the picture on my knee. It took only a few minutes to record the general idea, with written annotations of colours etc., before stowing the pad back in the map-pocket and pouring on the coal to get home again before dark.

The 'Guard's Club' – Lake Albert

Oil on board 34″ x 42″
Painted at Murchison Falls 1959
Repaired and restored, London 1984

There are no elephants left with tusks like this, anywhere in Africa today – but this picture has another story in its own right.

It was commissioned in the late fifties by Col Leon Jones JP, to be presented to Uganda National Parks, so that prints from it could be sold to raise funds for conservation. It was to be a tribute to the 'Lord Mayor of Paraa,' an irrascible old elephant with a broken tusk and a volatile personality, who had wrought much local havoc and finally had to be shot. The affection he had attracted through his antics, however, lingered on.

When I arrived at Murchison Falls to join the Warden, John Savidge, and met some of the Parks Trustees in Entebbe, they all said I should forget the Lord Mayor as a posthumous model and insisted he be remembered by 'real' elephants. Go and find the 'Guards Club' at Buligi, they said.

Buligi is an area of open savannah country much like parts of our South Downs with short, dry grass, sweeping cloud-shadows, and beyond it Lake Albert and the Congo hills growing great cauliflowers of thunder cloud in the midday heat. Then I saw the 'Club'.

They were all huge but one old bull more closely resembled a mastodon than an elephant, with tusks so long and heavy he would rest them on the ground and doze.

I was there for some weeks so there was ample time to sketch, plan the picture and paint it before going home. The prints were made in London and the original, imposingly framed, returned to hang in the Safari Lodge at Paraa. Soon after that came *uhuru* (freedom) and soon after that – Idi Amin. Uganda sadly, had fallen on hard times.

By the early eighties the Safari Lodge had been sacked and lay roofless to the elements. A visiting pilot from Nairobi landed one day on the airstrip, wandered round the deserted ruin and found this picture, still hanging crookedly on its nail with the frame smashed. There were spear gashes and bullet-holes through it – but it was in otherwise mint condition!

The picture was simply impounded, put aboard the aeroplane and flown back for safe keeping. Later I was asked if I could fix it and I promised to try.

British Airways flew it home and the framemaker in London repaired the frame. And there was I with my Polyfilla – a helpful material about the home but seldom perhaps, for this particular purpose, filling the holes and 'making good.' This complete, I carefully painted over the repairs and restored the picture to its original appearance.

This experience, more than any other, confirmed my faith in hardboard as a painting surface. For years I had blessed its versatility and durability and can now proclaim it the best of all if you plan to hang a picture where bullets are flying.

If there is any purely artistic consideration in all this, it must lie in the interpretation of so decisive a comment on a picture. Was it unrestrained disgust – or was it a statement of deep appreciation?

In the Heat of the Day – Thomson's Gazelles

Oil on board 24″ x 30″ (1960)
Published by Solomon & Whitehead

East Africa in the dry season has a unique magic which I felt strongly enough to want to 'capture'. The way to do it, I thought, was through the medium of typical wild animals in close association with the plains that support them.

It was a forlorn hope but worth a try and an obvious starting point was to choose one of the commonest, but also one of the loveliest of all Africa's animals, Thomson's gazelles. Impala may have more grace and elegance in movement, coupled with subtle, lyrate curvature of their heads but they lack bold markings. It was the 'Tommies' I wanted – urchin friskyness, strikingly marked bodies and faces, gently curved, heavily corrugated horns.

The colours of these animals, delineated and emphasised in candy stripes on forms that seem never to be still for a second, looked as good a way as any to attempt that elusive quality they call 'movement' and the most essential ingredient of the atmosphere I sought. (My old art teacher would at least have been proud of the attempt.)

Putting several animals together should take the exercise a stage further. The hope was that the general flow of one, would be taken up and continued by its neighbour and thus transmitted through the whole little group, goading them along.

Their colours, especially in sunlight, are hot and suggestive of the shimmering heat of the day. The grass must be golden, brittle and parched in the hope of adding a hint of rustle to whatever the gazelles could achieve for me. But all this is just high-falutin' prose which creeps inevitably into any description of pictures and their hidden motives – both by artists themselves and their even more voluble critics. Art is certainly a godsend for the verbose.

In real fact, I am the only one able to relate what I was trying to do and how I was trying to do it. In fairness I can say that it got some of the way there and was certainly worth trying. The magic of East Africa's dry season remains unattained and my attempted 'movement' all but ground to a halt.

Pinkfeet at Cloud Height

Oil on board 48″ x 72″ (1961)

A bond is established between an aviator and whatever birds are aloft beside or below him. In addition, to be feeling the same thumps of turbulence and unseen disquiet in the air that they know by birthright, has a way of cutting him down to size.

Theirs is the perfection of instinct, his the ham-handed gaucherie of a trespasser into another's element and made possible only with an intrusive piece of machinery. I must admit to similar feelings of inadequacy, awe and respect when under water, in the close and welcoming company of fishes and whales.

Despite an awareness of personal shortcomings, there is no denying the glow of achievement. The machine after all, has made possible the bird's own view of birds. If it is an intrusion, then it is short-lived. The birds are not the object of a chase, they have merely offered a glimpse of their less publicised movements, allowed a diffident and appreciative guest to accompany them for a few moments of their migration in their private element, and at the height they themselves have chosen, to suit the weather of the day.

VC-10 – Nocturne

Oil on board 30" x 40" (1962)

At the time this picture was painted, the leading patrons, especially for subjects like this, came from industry, with aeroplane manufacturers and fuel companies in the lead.

As a legacy of the war perhaps, aeroplanes had acquired strong devotees. Those who liked to paint as well, made aeroplanes their subject and the industry in turn, commissioned their work. Two memorable names stood out then, Frank Wootton and Roy Nockolds, both of whom had painted the flying scene throughout the War. But there were many others and they all came together when the Society of Aviation Artists was formed in 1954 and held its inaurgural exhibition at the Guildhall Art Gallery in London.

Frank Wootton was elected as the Founding President and has remained so thereafter, following the Society's name change to the Guild of Aviation Artists. The Guild continues to flourish today, fuelled by new enthusiasms, new young painters and new happenings in the air.

This picture was commissioned by a company that achieved lasting fame, Vickers-Armstrongs, later the British Aircraft Corporation. The shapely aircraft was the prototype VC-10, seen in bright moonlight – an imaginary nocturne. To me it was an imaginary aeroplane too, so much so that I was loaned a model of it which stood on the table at the chosen angle as one might place a wine bottle and a plate of aubergines for an exercise in still life.

If there is one problem that aeroplanes present to an artist, it is the impossibility of conveying by anything more than skilful artifice, its passage through the air. In essence it must remain a fixed shape superimposed on a background. The only choice is the angle from which it is viewed and its size in relation to the picture as a whole.

Thus the viewer must meet the artist halfway, allowing sympathy for the subject to take it all as read and accept that this uncompromising piece of machinery is actually moving with speed, through the medium for which it was designed.

The prototype was a success, with the success repeated by the production VC-10s in service. I am ashamed to relate that it was a different story for the model placed in my care. Its appeal to my young boys was too great to resist and it became a write-off even before the picture was finished!

Elephants and Piapiacs

Oil on board 30" x 24" (1963)

Very often with a painting, there is one dominant quality or direction of interest in the subject that determines everything. In the case of this one it was texture.

The elephants had sauntered up from the Nile and were quietly socialising in a dried-up swamp. By and large, elephants are the colour of what they last rolled in and they retain it, lightening in tone as it dries, until they next bathe. These elephants, having taken their time up the slope, were still clean but dusted perhaps, with a talcum of red laterite and this to a certain extent, echoed the colour of the mud in the drying swamp.

But it was texture, not colour, that claimed all the attention. The crazy-paving cracks in the mud were a perfect large-scale replica of the elephants' hide, and the hide in turn presented variations of finer and coarser textures according to the anatomy of the animals. The deep transverse ridges across the base of the trunks contrasted sharply with the smooth leather-like quality of the ears and the brow.

Finally, as if the whole texture theme needed the ultimate emphasis, came the tusks. Ivory will hold the stains of vegetable matter and river mud even after washing, so they tend to be a peaty brown or amber yellow. If one were committed to a search for total verisimilitude perhaps they should have been painted that way – but with a brush in hand and few scruples, what is the purpose of accepting dirty, sub-standard tusks on one's elephants? I have to admit to cleaning them up enough to make them a true accent against all those varied and rather abrasive surfaces in differing shades of brown. Their curves of course helped. On some animals tusks can be distorted or even broken off. I must confess also to preferring tusks that display that kind of sweet and pleasing parabola that could have come straight from the drawing-board of a naval architect.

There was, however, one last accent available and one that went beyond simply textural interest – the piapiacs.

Piapiacs are really just black magpies and display all our native magpie's gregariousness and bravado. Their distribution across West Africa and into Uganda exactly coincides with the borassus palm which sustains them as a breeding species. Where the palms abound, so do the birds. Where there are no borassus palms, piapiacs are absent. The palms are a vital host tree for many other life forms.

So the added garnish of the picture with piapiacs, locates the scene geographically, it adds a texture even smoother than ivory and of the very opposite colour – not just black but iridescent black with an added green or violet sheen. Moreover, young piapiacs have red bills, so it is nothing if not logical that the young and brighter birds would be chosen for this piece of animal interplay, emphasising in the process the contrasting demeanour – the dignity and gravitas of elephant kind with the bumptiousness of these birds.

Ash Trees at Tournebury

Oil on board 30″ x 24″ (1963)

For thirty-five years we lived in a cottage overlooking a creek of Chichester Harbour. The cottage backed on to Tournebury Woods, the site of an Iron Age camp dating from 500 BC.

A short walk from the back door took one over the moat and ramparts of the old 'bury,' under the wood's tallest oaks and beeches, all cluttered with heron's nests, then out on to the fresh marsh behind. Overlooking the marsh was this stand of ash trees.

Through their trunks and across the marsh, one saw the sea-wall angling away northwards, marking the foreshore. At high tide there was the blue of the sea with the occasional accent of a sail. Far beyond was the high ground of West Sussex, Kingley Vale and the South Downs. The ash trees in this light, seemed always to be masquerading as eucalyptus and a perpetual reminder of Australia.

Off Soundings

Oil on board 18″ x 24″ (1964)

This scene was painted just two years before Francis Chichester set out in *Gipsy Moth IV* to sail round the world alone. He was in his mid-sixties and the voyage, with its many dramas, lasted 226 days. He returned to Plymouth and a national ovation – later to be deservedly knighted by the Queen.

The picture itself belongs to my brother-in-law, Charles Whitehead, and is always thought of in the family as a tribute to Sir Francis. However, the vessel in the moonlight is not *Gipsy Moth* – she was a ketch. It is an imaginary one, the result of Francis Chichester sharing his plans and ambitions and in the process, conjuring up this image of a small yacht and a single-handed sailor, tramping along through the night, in optimum conditions – and miles off soundings.

Crowned Cranes

Opposite: Oil on board 24″ x 40″ (1967)
Above: Oil on board 24″ x 36″

T here are shapely birds like terns and pretty birds like goldfinches. There are colourful birds like macaws and flamboyant birds like peacocks. There are even endearingly ugly ones like marabou storks and vultures and all these adjectives relate to nothing more than physical appearance. They suggest how artists might view contrasting birds as subjects for their pictures and thereby raise the popular but steadfastly unanswerable question, 'Which would you name the most "beautiful" bird of all?'

For my part it is 'beauty' itself that needs the explanation. Does this elusive quality lie in the body form, the grace of movement, the adornments of seemingly extraneous plumage or the intricacies of pattern and colour? How for instance, does a woodcock compare in beauty terms, with an egret? I have thought about this a lot, if only in the belief that there might be (perhaps) a viable answer. Once I even thought I had it.

This optimism lay in the possible introduction of an entirely new, up-to-the-minute, adjective – 'designer'. We have 'designer' clothes, even (some of us) 'designer' stubble on our chins. 'Designer' goods are everywhere, so why not a 'designer' bird? And if there were such a thing, I have not the slightest doubt it would have to be the crowned crane.

Instead of coming about through eons of mystical evolution and natural selection, the crowned crane looks to me more like a spectacular short-cut to instant elegance, and if that were not sufficient, elegance embellished with a flawless colour scheme.

It almost suggests a product of *human* creation; from the drawing-board of a free-range artistic fantasist of super-human taste and discernment.

The message it proclaims is that someone, somewhere, has found a means of isolating all the multifarious ingredients of beauty and distilling them into a single design – a 'designer' design. The prototype would then have received a blessing from on high and the crowned crane put into mass production.

But an answer to the unavoidable question is still elusive as ever and every bit as fascinating. *Is* the designer bird any more beautiful than the shapely tern – or is this just another case of back to the drawing-board?

Cruiser on the High Sand

Oil on board 18″ x 36″ (1964)

The high sand depicted in this painting is Stocker Sands and many, having come to rest upon it with no intention of so doing, have greeted the event with appropriate expletives. There is then little to pass the time except for the hope that the next tide will be high enough to refloat the vessel and that the benign weather will hold for its arrival.

Some victims of this error of judgement will embark upon what zoologists call 'displacement activity.' This consists of making much play with scrubbers and scrapers, to sell the idea to passers-by in the deep water channel, that the grounding was deliberate – with the intention of attending to the offending barnacles on her bottom. Others are seen to react in a more stoical fashion – perhaps because there are no scrapers on board.

Few I suspect, will concern themselves with the thought that a well-designed yacht at an angle like this, offers a spectacle of considerable delight to anyone with an eye for shape – and a delight made greater by memories of having done precisely the same thing oneself.

'Chiquita'

Oil on board 24" x 18" (1969)

Though I have never flown a hawk myself, in a parasitic sort of way I have passed a lot of time drawing and painting the birds my friends have owned and trained. It was a chance not to be missed – an intimate, eyeball-to-eyeball study session with some of the most impressive birds that fly. Being right-handed I could take the 'model' on my left fist, squat down and draw away with the pad on my knee.

I could never tire of the company of falconers, their language (and sometimes their dress) comes straight from Chaucer, but their enthusiasm for all things wild and for wilderness places is nourishment in itself. Watching them fly their birds and handle their traditional 'furniture' (the hoods, jesses, bells and gloves), swinging the lure and taking up their falcon, is like planting oneself in the best seat at a royal performance with no inkling of the patience and the grind that goes into rehearsal.

This is a portrait of 'Chiquita', owned by an old friend, Tony Foster. She was his first peregrine and his favourite. She was known as 'Chiquita' because she came from Spain and is of the race of *Falco peregrinus* called *Brookii*, the Mediterranean race.

Tony and a mutual friend, Dick Treleven, an avid painter and lover of falcons, were flying 'Chiquita' at rooks in Cornwall, when she was lost (it happens easily) and much anxiety followed. She had been loose on Bodmin Moor for eleven days when Dick heard of her whereabouts, alerted her owner and she was taken up in a happy reunion.

'Chiquita's' life, though short, was eventful and rewarding. She had flown during the 1961 Game Fair at Weston Park in falconry demonstrations and overflown some of the loveliest highground in the south-west. Sadly, she died of aspergillosis, a disease brought on by infection from fungal spores in decaying vegetation – an unfitting end to be sure, for so dynamic a creature.

41

Cormorants on the Wreck Structure

Oil on board 30" x 24" (1968)

The uncompromising geometry of man-made artefacts when involved with the freer lines of living creatures has always appealed to me. The contrast it presents is irresistibly striking. Examples of this can be seen every day – a kestrel on a telegraph pole, a sparrow on a barbed-wire fence, gulls resting on a seaside roof-top. In this picture it is a convocation of cormorants, perched and drying wings on a wreck-marking structure off Brightlingsea. This sort of green is always used when denoting wrecks or obstructions, so it even brings an essentially artificial *colour* into the equation, adding a further accent to its incongruity.

For me however, this picture is always remembered by an unusual accolade it once drew from a critic as it hung in an exhibition at London's Guildhall Art Gallery.

I had noticed the critic, who was in fact, the reigning President of the RSMA, appraising the picture in thoughtful silence. Academic hands grasped his jacket lapels, his head was slightly back and tilted to one side with the lips pursed. He was simply adopting the accepted stance we all emulate when seeking to pass ourselves off as sage and well-informed in matters of art.

As I drew alongside he completed the act by emitting the sound that can denote either appreciation or misgivings with equal ease. – a drawn out sigh like the collapse of a party balloon.

'Do you like it?' I asked.

His lips still pursed, he swivelled his eyes to me over the rims of his spectacles.

'Do you know Keith,' he replied with deep sincerity, 'I don't think there is another painter in Europe today, who displays quite your panache in the rendering of birdshit.'

Fulmar Courtship – Godrevy Head

Oil on board 24″ x 18″ (1967)

In a very real way, fulmars are vest-pocket albatrosses. They are designed for the open ocean, are out there year-round and come ashore only to breed. Seeing them close-up and on dry land, it is immediately apparent that a life-long habit of rakish and enduring flight, has done little to foster their agility on foot.

Like true pelagic creatures, they pick the furthest outposts of the land, the high cliffs and off-shore skerries, and bring to them some of their own magic – the feeling of a seafarer's homecoming.

To share this one must be prepared for a scramble – and also keep one's distance. A well-aimed squirt of warm stomach oil can render one socially unwelcome for days to come.

Their courtship clamour is loud and urgent, their pair-bonding gestures of affection, gentle and touching in every meaning of the word. But in a fulmar's life this is a short, if necessary, seasonal break in a haphazardly itinerant, undisturbed and virtually silent life, well off the shores of the North Atlantic.

43

Black-tailed Godwits and the Flood Tide

Oil on board 18″ x 48″ (1974)

The most rewarding piece of loot that came my way after the War (with official sanction) was an enormous pair of bridge binoculars from a German destroyer. A friend had mounted them for me, on a mahogany tripod that had once supported a surveyor's theodolite. The item when fully assembled, was, and still is, both monstrously heavy and quite indispensable. Originally there had been a range-finding graticule built into the field of view. This I had removed, leaving an uncluttered disc of perfect clarity and steady as a rock.

Every day, especially during the spring and autumn migrations, I would carry this item on my shoulder and a note-book in my pocket, out to the point beyond our cottage, plant it three-leggedly and well-splayed and sweep the harbour with its all-seeing powers. Because the eye pieces face upwards, the observer is looking down. The eyes can therefore flick from a far-away subject to the pencil on paper and back again (without batting an eyelid seems appropriate). One can stand there and, quite literally, draw from life with the eyes and pencil the only things in motion.

Some traumatic sights must have passed through those prisms between 1939 and 1945, but what I have seen since, I feel, has made amends.

In the warm days of late summer the first black-tailed godwits would arrive, their breeding plumage still intact – an arresting flash of chestnut red out on the flats. More would follow, sometimes in their thousands. Some would stay the winter, others moved on south.

While they were around, however, they were *the* subject, translated from life into pages and pages of crude, pin-man attitude sketches and finally into paint with an attempt at organisation and arrangement. Most of all I liked to make long pictures of them – long enough to gauge the depth of the incoming tide against their stately legs and knobbly knees, as the eyes move along their little group.

I love the way they face like weathercocks into the breeze; acting as living indicators of all that is going on in a world of captivating inconstancy, where wind and tide and these alone are joint masters.

The First Arrivals –
Black-tailed Godwits

Oil on board 18″ x 30″ (1968)

MS *Lindblad Explorer*

Oil on board 24″ x 36″ (1970)

There is much I am unhappy about in this picture but it does, none the less, stand as a milestone and for that reason, if no other, must be included.

Artistically I think it is rather 'over the top', though in a well-meaning way. I was so besotted about this vessel that I tried to make her look imposing instead of the endearingly unlovely little thing she was. I then cluttered her up with bizarre ice shapes drawn all over the place and set her in front of a famous Antarctic landscape, which I proceeded to distort as greviously as the ship.

From all this it will be apparent that I am a little less than happy today with a picture which at the time it was painted, twenty-seven years ago, I had thought rather impressive. In all honesty, however, it must be said that this applies to other pictures of mine, both in this book and in the world at large. That is the way it goes.

The ship herself, *Lindblad Explorer*, was indeed a milestone in her own right and affected many others as well as me. She was the very first purpose-built, go-anywhere ship to be designed and built from the keel up for what has now become known as 'Exploration Cruising.' For years she was the only ship of her kind on the high seas and ever since she sailed south on her maiden voyage in 1969, I had the good fortune to be aboard for a few months each year, filling a post euphemistically referred to as 'naturalist,' keeping the wildlife log and driving one of her Zodiac landing boats. In this way her presence must be accepted as the means of fulfilment behind many of the subsequent pictures in this book – Arctic, Antarctic and oceanic islands between the two.

Her litany of achievements and minor discoveries are told in *Ship in the Wilderness*, illustrated with some of my drawings but in the main, by sensational photographs by a shipmate from California, Jim Snyder. For this reason I shall not cover the same ground here but passage of years now calls for a short epilogue. She is still afloat and still working the wilderness. Her name, after a change or two, is simply MS *Explorer. Ship in the Wilderness* had been dedicated to Lars-Eric Lindblad, 'who dreamed her up and made her happen.' He died in Sweden in 1994 and is greatly missed – but his torch burns on.

In the old days her passengers joined her as a working, oceanographic vessel, equipped with winches for handling plankton nets, a small laboratory with microscopes for marine biology and a crow's nest wired to the bridge for conning her through pack-ice. She was comfortable but no gin palace. Some years ago she underwent an extensive refit following a change of ownership. A new philosophy had dawned with priorities on comfort rather than purpose and the 'cruise ship' image settled upon her.

During the maiden voyage I had painted a mural of Adelie penguins waddling down to the water's edge, on the forward bulkhead of the little lecture theatre cum laboratory. This too became a casualty of the big face-lift and caused much grief among her old passengers. I have to admit that it was never one of my favourite works and compared with the loss of the crow's nest, a slight of very minor proportions. I was touched however, to find my loyal friends and shipmates regarding it as little short of vandalism.

I shall always remember her as the pioneer, the source of lasting friendships and the opener of a thousand doors. That is why she is a milestone.

Southern Ocean – Storm Force Ten

Oil on board 24″ x 48″ (1987)

Wandering Albatross

Oil on board 24″ x 30″ (1990)

Gentoo Penguins

Oil on board 18″ x 48″ (1986)

In the years that followed the launch of *Lindblad Explorer* something like an inspirational dam must have burst. Subjects I had always longed to paint but had never even seen, began parading constantly before my eyes. The seventies and eighties were certainly the most prolific painting years I remember, despite being away from home and the studio for many months in every year.

Homecomings began a frenzy of catching up, consolidating ideas and images that had become dangerously explosive in their cooped-up need for expression. Sometimes I managed to clear the slate, other times I failed. With a pile of loose ends still untied, I was packing gear once again for the next commitment and would be off to rejoin my home-from-home in some enticing little port on the other side of the world.

Within five years of her launching it was true to say that *Lindblad Explorer* had seen more of the untrodden corners of the oceans, than any ship afloat. Because she is still at it, the claim would be true today – despite an armada of other vessels, large and small, that have taken up her challenge and followed in her wake.

But it will always be Antarctica that I see as her stage. It was as if the siren-song of the world's greatest and most enduring wilderness had claimed her. She was allowed to be Antarctica's summer guest, but such hospitality can only be short-lived, so she wandered the world as if filling in time before the South called her eagerly back in the next austral spring.

The paintings that follow demand little in the way of explanation and share the same background story. They are simply examples of the material this ship was offering – to be used in whatever way an observer might find fulfilling or appropriate.

A kittiwake following in her quarter-wave, was probably my earliest memory, on her way from Southampton to Madeira, on the first leg of what proved to be an eventful maiden voyage.

In the south latitudes albatrosses were waiting to take over as her escort. I cannot think how many times I have watched their flight as if for the first time, and resolved to go home and paint it, oblivious of the fact that it is not the first time and certainly will not be the last. It is no more than expressing the hope that on this occasion, I will get that little bit nearer to justice for so compelling a subject.

The sobering enormity of gales at sea, one's faith in the Divine and a stalwart ship were a big part of it all. The ocean south of Cape Horn gave daily lessons in both the structure of waves and their movement and in personal humility. It was a drama one could never walk out on and go below. The star was always on stage and the star was the albatross, wings cranked against the screaming wind, sweeping about in some exultant show of exuberance while savouring some inner peace that borders on disdain for the fury of the sea.

The toast of any voyage was 'First Ice' – harbinger of the great white continent. There would be ice in plenty to come but never another first. And so it was with penguins. Their noise, their smell and their sheer numbers would later become accepted. But the memory of the first little group one's eyes had ever seen, stumbling along like laundry bags on the move, over some outlying ice-floe, would surely last forever.

I thank that little ship for all this. There were other ships to follow and they too, became means to an end that emerged in paint and provided great joy of living along the way. But as with the first penguins, the first polar ship will always hold precedent in memory.

Kittiwake in the Quarter-wave

Oil on board 24" x 48" (1971)

Portrait of an Iceberg

Oil on board 18" x 24" (1990)

In Paradise Bay – Antarctic Terns below the Glacier

Oil on board 18" x 24" (1978)

Paradise Bay lies at about 65 degrees south, on the west side of the Antarctic Peninsula and I have searched in vain through the *Antarctic Pilot* and gazetteers of Antarctic place names, in the hope of discovering when, and by whom, it found its name.

It was clearly named for no mortal sailor, nor is it likely to have been named for his ship. Paradise Bay it may be safely assumed, was named by an admirer, for itself – and with every justification. The number of times I have heard eulogies like 'whoever named this place must have arrived on a day like this,' testifies to a lasting reputation for weather of the most celestial clemency.

Fair weather, when present in this part of the world, is more accurately described as 'beautiful.' A clear, soundless, anticyclonic calm, under brilliant and near-perpetual sunshine becomes the pattern which can hold for days, even weeks.

Great icebergs and distant mountains with their upside-down images rise from a sea as blue as a kingfisher's wing. Tiny storm petrels, hanging on fluttering wings, bounce about the surface, stirring up the reflections with out-stretched paddles in search of floating nourishment too small to see. A seal will surface, glance around and drop from sight. Sometimes, ridiculously close at hand, a whale announces its presence with a great, blasting breath and slides on down with scarcely a ripple, still clearly visible under water like a magnificent submarine, leaving on the air the lingering effluvium of the inner whale – a reminder that a mighty mammal just passed this way.

Paradise Bay calls for a sacred, cathedral-type of silence, so people talk in whispers if they need to talk at all – and even then may expect a reproachful finger laid against the lips by anyone in earshot.

Sounds that come across the water are the tuning-up of a natural orchestra: the exhaling whale, a distant clamour of penguins, blue-eyed shags at their nests in the shelter of an overhung cliff with Antarctic terns shrieking above them and raucous kelp gulls circling.

On these warm, Paradise days, one often hears the roar of an avalanche far up in the mountainous spine of the Peninsula and closer at hand, the glacier fronts releasing a few hundred tons of ice straight into the bay. Then the sleeping reflections are rudely awakened and jostle in confusion until soothed back once more into the pattern of idyllic, sunlit, peace.

It is perverse I suppose, to wax so lyrical on the joys of such surroundings, while side-stepping them so often when it comes to paint. Justified or not, the explanation is simple. Like flamboyant sunsets, rose-tinted alps and golden, autumn woods, they are something for living in rather than painting. I find my courage ebbs and the exercise a little pre-sumptuous. In the same way, conditions that would be made-to-measure for a French ski resort brochure, or a golfing hotel in Bermuda, become something of a cliché when translated into paint.

The result is that I have never painted this gorgeous place in the mood it so often and so honestly presents, but several times in the reverse or some sort of halfway stage. This is when a hint of inclemency shows itself, pro-claiming that despite all its connotations of Paradise, this place is just another piece of Antarctica – the continent that is savage and unrelenting, yet infinitely beautiful in every mood of a repertoire without limit.

Perpetual sunshine I concluded, is fine to live under (for a while) but it offers little in the way of real, visual excitement. It will strip any landscape of its subtleties and thrust its nakedness into your face. The real allure comes with what is half-seen. Paradise Bay, at least through the eye of a painter, comes into its own with the bitter winds and the mists and the half-light – and every other kind of weather our natural instincts tell us to avoid.

Bridled Terns – Desroches Atoll

Oil on board 24" x 30" (1972)

The pattern of operation for MS *Lindblad Explorer*, was to work in the Antarctic through the southern summer – roughly November to March. This was her busiest time in any year. From about July until the early autumn she was in the Arctic. Like the Arctic tern she had to get from one to the other and back again and it was those little interludes en route that provided memorable and often unexpected rewards.

It could be the Atlantic or the Pacific and even then the detailed itineraries were wonderfully variable. Apart from regulars like the Amazon, she seldom became involved in any one tropical area for any length of time.

In the early '70s however, her first years afloat, there was an exception. She spent about three months based on Mombasa with the Seychelles her major destination. There was no airport on Mahé then and in consequence, the Seychelles were very different from today.

Before returning to Mombasa she would visit the Amirante Islands, Cosmoledo and Aldabra, the Comores and sometimes Madagascar and Zanzibar, even then varying the island ports of call and extending the experience of all on board. Serious zoologists and marine biologists on the staff derived great value from this and were able to compile regular records of happenings during that period, on islands that were otherwise hardly ever seen.

There are few things in life which give me greater happiness than walking the beach of a *truly* uninhabited island, where there are no human footprints whatever but one's own. When I could escape from duties in such a place, I would try to walk all the way round. It might take half a day or less than an hour.

Islands that took a whole day tended to be inhabited and not withstanding the loveliness of those shore-based people, there were lovely people on board too. It was a little escape I needed – just to recharge the batteries. After that, and for a few days more, I could be as lovely as the next man.

It was in the course of one of these little private 'hookies' that I came upon this group of bridled terns resting on driftwood and this picture was conceived.

Islands in the Trade Wind belts have a similarity entirely bestowed by the wind. On the lee side the sea laps gently. The wind in the coconut palms and the casuarinas is distant so that bird calls clearly reach the ears. The lull lasts until the beach begins curving round to windward, or reaches a decisive point when all at once the shelter is lost, the wind is there again, strong and refreshing and a lively surf is crashing onto the shore.

A point, like this one on Desroches can be second heaven to the dedicated beachcomber, with the whole spectrum of maritime offerings at your feet. The undamaged shell of an argonaut catches the eye, or even a paper nautilus, green glass floats from the Japanese long-liners – and further down the scale of visual desirability, plastic sandals, light bulbs, squeezy bottles and dismembered dolls – flotsam and jetsam of the high seas from which no island or remote coastline is spared.

Each island seems to have one favoured area where the lion's share of the wind-garnered harvest is concentrated and retained. Jostled and burnished by the surf, it has been thrown up high and clear to dry and bleach out in the sun. Artistically the most appealing is the driftwood, now resolved by weathering into simple shapes and folds like giant monuments of pasta erected on a plinth of sand.

One thing only can be permitted to embellish so perfect a piece of sculpture – and that is something from the same origins, something like seabirds.

Time passed unnoticed with my bridled terns so appropriately displayed, that I had to finish my circuit at a run, leap into my boat, and race back to the ship to be in time to avoid a stern reprimand – in Norwegian.

As it transpired all the lovely people were happily back aboard and mostly in the bar – lovely as ever. And thanks to the terns I felt pretty lovely too.

Coral, Coachmen and Sergeant-Majors

Oil on board 24″ x 36″ (1972)

If coral is the flower-garden, then fishes are the butterflies. The principal characters in this picture here, are *Heniochus acuminatus*, sometimes called long-finned butterflyfish or, by virtue of their whip, 'coachmen.' The ubiquitous sergeant-majors are those in lower key, with more muted stripes.

No painter could resist the sort of subjects the undersea can provide, especially the reefs where the flower garden erupts in 'plants' that would have delighted Salvador Dali. At tropical noon with the sun high above, light falls uncompromisingly on the moving shapes, shading one and illuminating the next, laying a halo round body forms and glowing from back-lit fins. Distance is resolved into a diorama, like a stage-set designed for the Ziegfeld Follies with the entire cast of thousands wearing pyjamas.

Denizens of reefs are very local. They tend to live their whole lives within a foot or two of a single coral feature, while the feature itself enjoys an altogether new display of activity with the setting of the sun. The coachmen then will hide away as the night-shift wakes up in the darkness.

This fish is one of my favourites. There is genuine dignity in their movements, as if their name referred only to coachmen in royal employment.

They go a little way then stop, as though for a chat with colleagues and I grouped them this way to stress a collective bond with their own little plot. Reefs, in terms of bio-diversity, are the richest environments on earth, and paradoxically, the most vulnerable. A good fish-watcher will record on a healthy reef, ninety species or more in the duration of a single tank of air. In the same time a good birder, if lucky, might see nine species along the island shore. This scene is a gift beyond price. It is something that man, but for the ingenuity of his inventions, was never intended to look upon.

Tiger

Oil on board 30″ x 18″ (1973)

Published as Limited Edition Print by Mill Pond Press Inc., Florida 1981

The impact any animal has on someone seeing it for the first time depends on age, experience and preconceptions. I was five when I saw my first whale. Leaning over the rails of a ship out of Cape Town, bound for Perth, Australia, I watched five or six of them (blue whales at that) and remember being disappointed because they were actually *smaller* than the 22,000-ton ship.

On the same voyage I saw my first albatross and felt let down because it failed to darken the sun. Based upon fanciful stories I had expected something more in line with a Boeing 747. Happily those first impressions have readjusted themselves during the 45 years it took before I found myself face to face with a wild tiger while on a film assignment in India. The sight was from the back of an elephant.

There can not be a child over four who will not recognise a tiger on the instant and say its name. They must be the most familiar of all animals, from books, zoos and even circuses. We take them for granted as a large and legendary version of the prowling cat with the infinitely flexible, boneless body, powered only by sinews. But we are perceiving them out of context. Where they belong, where they reign over their natural domain, they are something else.

The wild tiger comes as a vision, a heart-stopping apparition for which inexplicably, one is unprepared. It commands a 'presence' that I have experienced with no other animal, a presence that stays with it until it vanishes as though it were part of the aura of the animal itself. It is something calling more for total admiration than fear. And what remains is an everlasting sense of privilege at having looked upon the most sensationally beautiful quadruped on earth.

Temple-Haunting Parakeets – Khajuraho

Oil on board 24″ x 12″ (1973)

The Paraswantha Temple at Khajuraho has been aptly described as the triumph of sculpture over architecture. It is an extravaganza of intricate stone carvings that cover an entire building and have withstood the weathering of a thousand years.

Ever since the Mediaeval Hindu Renaissance, this lady has held her serene expression while touching up her eye-lashes with black surma. Then the parakeets arrived.

Raucously oblivious to her presence as anything more than something to perch on, fight around and nest behind, they presented a stunning contrast of demeanour, let alone of colour.

The lady had time on her hands, so I sketched her after the birds had gone. The fleeting spectacle of the parakeets themselves was already committed to memory, helped later by reference to parakeets elsewhere and brought together in an attempt to recreate a lovely but short-lived moment.

Chamois on the Rothorn

Oil on board 36″ x 24″ (1969)

Here was an attempt to introduce a note of vertigo, so the inevitable first decision was to plan an upright format for the picture. The chamois subjects were in plenty on the Rothorn in 1969 and in pursuit of my vertigo quest, I instinctively put two of them in at the top – peering downwards. The angles delineating snow and rock were to be as acute as reason would permit and the cornice in the top left-hand corner needed to look a little insecure against the beckoning finger of gravity.

To harmonise the composition I felt that there had to be a consequential shape towards the bottom of the picture, just where the wedge-shaped patch of snow widens out. A rock might have done it but another chamois, I thought, would do better – by introducing a rather fascinating phenomenon. A viewer of a picture will follow, perhaps unconsciously, the line of interest indicated by the character *in* the picture – to look where he, she, or they are looking to find the target of all the attention.

So the chamois at the bottom is now looking up to his friends above. The viewer follows the animal's gaze only to see them returning the glance. It becomes an up and down journey for the eye of the viewer. Furthermore the angle is very steep and accentuated by the straight, uncompromising line of the snow's profile.

All in all, it is a landscape built on end and one in which chamois are clearly content. But then I suppose the effects of vertigo, whether seen as an aim for a picture or a fact of life, would cut little ice with a chamois.

61

Mount Erebus

Oil on board 18″ x 24″ (1974)

'With a favourable breeze, and very clear weather, we stood to the southward, close to some land which had been in sight since the preceeding noon and which we then called the 'High Island.' It proved to be a mountain 12,400 feet of elevation above the level of the sea, emitting flames and smoke in great profusion; at first the smoke appeared like snow-drift, but as we drew nearer, its true character became manifest.

'The discovery of an active volcano in so high a southern latitude cannot but be esteemed a circumstance of high geological importance and interest, and contribute to throw some further light on the physical construction of our globe. I named it "Mount Erebus" . . .'

From the Log of HMS *Erebus*. Captain Sir James Clark Ross, 28 January 1841

S ince its discovery this mountain has dominated the stage set for the 'heroic age' of Antarctic exploration. It features generously in the notes and even the drawings of those very special men – and its magic lingers on.

There is no longer 'flame and smoke in great profusion' though she is very positively active. Some days Ross's 'smoke that appeared like snow-drift' would still apply but one would need to look down into the depths of the crater itself to see fire.

She may not be the highest but she is certainly Antarctica's most famous mountain and I say 'she' not from any suggestion that volcanos in general have a feminine persona – just that this particular one was named after a ship!

Elephant and Baobab Tree

Oil on board 24" x 36" (1976)

Today the world is awash with brilliant wildlife photographers but not so long ago there was just a handful of household names and amongst them was Eric Hosking. He was, and still is, revered as a doyen of the profession and famous images from his camera, even from his first brassbound mahogany one that you could scarcely lift, still keep appearing despite the pressures of present-day competition.

But Eric was a true patron of the arts, with a passion for paintings. By the time he reached eighty there was scarcely a square inch of wall space in his house for more.

Because he had a foot in each camp as it were, his views and arguments on the relative status of paint-brushes and cameras were much in demand. They were always stimulating and often hilarious. His leg was pulled about his resentment that painters could 'readjust' a subject with limitless freedom while he was forced to snap up whatever fate had put on offer. He would even recall wistfully, his early days when he was roped in to photograph wedding groups and the like, 'because at least you could arrange your subjects in order of priority or size and tell them when to smile!'

Painter friends who secretly envied his camera skills, would taunt him for only seeing life through a view-finder. He knew this well and enjoyed the joke. One day we met a few weeks after he had returned from his first major safari. He pulled his own leg with an immortal comment, 'I've just come out of my dark-room – and I had no idea that Dorothy and I had seen so much in Africa.'

This picture of the elephant and the baobab tree, was a gift from Eric to his wife Dorothy, for whom these two manifestations of Africa had left the deepest impression. She is not alone. Both are arresting enough to qualify as trademarks for a whole continent. The baobab has to be the elephant's botanical counterpart. There is a wonderful visual empathy between them.

HMS *Bulwark*

Oil on board 24" x 36" (1976)

In 1975 a stimulating assignment came my way. It was to join 45 Commando, Royal Marines, to paint a picture of their Arctic and Mountain Warfare training in north Norway – in winter. I came home with the happiest memories. When the picture was unveiled in the Mess at Arbroath, they even liked that too!

The sequel to which this experience gave rise, was both different and unexpected, though many of the same people were involved. This time the picture was for the Corps of Royal Marines and the subject was to be the Commando Carrier, HMS *Bulwark*.

I tend to feel a little uneasy about this kind of brief. It was on a technical level far over my head; everyone connected with it was not only encyclopedic in their knowledge but, I feared, determined that no civilian (especially of the 'creative' kind) would run rough-shod over their sacred bailiwicks. But I was soon put at ease. The armed services contain some of the most civilised, courteous and understanding people in the land. They had foreseen my possible concern and appointed one officer only to conduct the briefing for the picture and to approve it (or otherwise) when finished. He clearly enjoyed their full confidence. ('No committees please – or we'll be at it 'till Christmas!')

A week later, the Captain and I stood on *Bulwark*'s flight deck at Portsmouth. She was undergoing what is quaintly known as a DAMP (Dockyard Assisted Maintenance Period). Artistically, from where we stood, she resembled a long row of municipal tennis courts, threateningly overlooked by the technological equivalent of the Albert Memorial (actually the 'island') on which the gilt and gingerbread had been entirely replaced with mind-blowing electronics and armour plate – and painted grey. Just then, the prospect of making a picture out of any of this looked remote to say the least.

After her DAMP, however, I joined her in Gibraltar where 42 Commando were embarked and she set sail for Malta to take part in a NATO landing exercise.

My quarters were of the kind that can produce *folies de grandeur*. Somewhere inside the 'island' was a special cabin reserved for visiting admirals – a sort of duplicate bridge formed an annexe from which he could maintain contact with whatever operations were in hand. This time it was *I* who was the 'admiral.'

Later my personal Lynx helicopter took off from the flight deck and proceeded ahead of the ship as she steamed towards Malta. The Lynx turned and hovered and let me look back at the ship.

She looked magnificent. The first unpromising impressions at Portsmouth Dockyard had vanished. She was something entirely different. From this position, ahead and out on the starboard bow the tennis courts fell into striking perspective, so too was the 'Albert Memorial,' pleasingly asymmetrical to fulfil the whole purpose of the ship and almost overhanging the sea. The curving line of the stem swept away below the lip of the flight deck and where her forefoot sliced the sea a pair of dolphins had joined her as escort.

Later the exercise began, the flight deck was abuzz with activity and the routine with my own helicopter and personal pilot continued. Every question was answered, all the advice in the world was there for the taking and as with 45 Commando in the snow-covered mountains of Norway, it was an inspiring experience, though perhaps, with greater creature comforts.

Five days later it was all over and I savoured what was probably my last taste of being treated, no matter if misguidedly, as a VIP.

'Captain's compliments Mr Shackleton, and your helicopter is waiting on the flight deck. Your London flight has been alerted.'

My last memory of HMS *Bulwark* was her shapely, distinctive and now endearing bulk cruising off Malta, as I was delivered to the tarmac beside my flight to London – all formalities cleared – and bade a fond farewell.

Magnificent Frigatebirds

Oil on board 24″ x 36″ (c. 1976)

The ability of birds to fly brings aeronautical terms into descriptions of their aerial capabilities and frigatebirds have an important statistic which, to me, says everything about them. They have the lowest wing-loading of any bird. Their total body weight in relation to the area of their outstretched wings, is the lowest of all. The opposite extreme – highest wing-loading – belongs to the auks.

This imparts to the frigatebird's flight an amazing buoyancy and finger-tip control. They move effortlessly in the air, hanging on the wind, conjuring up comparisons with witches on broomsticks with their long forked tails, or visitations from the black angels of death. (Frigatebird similies tend to come on the sinister side.)

Not only is the wing lightly laden, it is markedly cranked in profile, rather bat-like, yet very deep in chord where it joins the body and the scapular feathers form an elongated fillet.

All in all it is a combination that offers the sweetest collection of curves both in the arrangement of flight feathers and in basic bone structure that is a pleasure to draw and is set off at its best in counterpoint with a background of guano-spattered thorn bushes.

It should also go without saying that the full extravaganza of shape, colour and exhibitionism is enshrined in the male. It is he who develops the crimson, inflatable gullar sac, extended to fully stretched translucency like a party balloon on the point of explosion, vibrating and wobbling in ecstatic frenzy as the fervour of courtship mounts.

This particular display of sexual rivalry is in the Galápagos Islands and these are the magnificent frigatebirds whose iridescent neck feathers cascade from the shoulders in the manner of a rooster's tail. Each suitor clearly believes in his own irresistibility – only the female shows discreet composure. She has seen it all before and reserves her right to be unimpressed.

There is however, just one male with the good sense to deflate and cut his losses . . .

Now I am well aware that in zoological circles, anthropomorphism is regarded as a sin level-pegging with aggravated theft, but one could be excused for looking upon this piece of interplay as a slice of life that has counterparts closer to home.

A Red-breast among the Brents

Oil on board 18" x 36" (1976)

It is a conditioned reflex among bird-people, that when faced with a huge flock of one species, they will automatically sift through it with dedicated intent; looking for something out of kilter with the crowd.

The harder it is to find, the greater is the joy of finding it. A few thousand dunlin, packed like shingle on a beach, might yield to the keen sighted, a curlew sandpiper. An acre or two of white-fronted geese grazing on the Slimbridge Dumbles, may offer up a solitary *lesser* white-fronted goose.

Here, the only sure distinction is its yellow eyelid! It is a feature that does not exactly advertise itself, but when found (and I have found it myself) other subtle differences can be noted in the bird, differences that in themselves would not be proof enough for positive identification. Some are even little mannerisms with social implications, of the kind one might expect of an individual of one species, surrounded by a few thousand of another.

This painting is of a visitor which, though infrequent, appears every few years, and generally in the compny of the very plentiful brents. Worldwide the red-breasted goose has a small population, with its wintering grounds in Romania and Bulgaria, along the west side of the Black Sea. That is where the mother lode of the species will be while this venturesome individual is visiting Britain.

When it does, it never goes unnoticed. It is definitely a high grade beginner's bird in the field of 'twitching.' Its arrival is an event often spotted a mile away and with the naked eye, like spotting an unexpected liquorice allsort in a barrow-load of acorns.

Here lies another form of bonus. Because the bird is so easy to find and once found, so hard to lose, it becomes a focal point of interest in its social interaction with the surrounding, uniform crowd. Generally they are smaller, this particular one was a little larger than most and this alone may have given him/her the self-confidence it plainly showed. Ahead of it, as it walked with its patrician gait, the brents would offer a fleeting show of deference. Behind its back, there would be a little more of the cautious bravado common to other sorts of animals in similar circumstances – including the uppermost primates!

Because it is instantly noticed, the arrival of a red-breasted goose always prompts the swiftest reaction from the birding world. It was only

a matter of hours before coaches began to come in from all over the land, cars, bumper-to-bumper, would line the coastal lanes. Along the sea-wall, tripods and telescopes were broken out in their hundreds and all with a single and very distinguished target.

If one needed to find the bird, one followed first the vehicles and then the direction of their occupants' gaze. It might be grazing on the winter wheat inland, or out on the mud, picking over the green entomorpha and sea lettuce. Wherever it was each day, it was easily found and this particular representative of the species had suddenly become (for the duration of its stay) the most famous *Branta ruficolis* in all the world.

Chesil Beach

Oil on board 18" x 24" (1977)

The Shell Calendar for 1979 featured 'Coastlines.' They had to be varied in character and represent all countries of the United Kingdom – otherwise the choice was left to me. Planning it all, with maps spread out on the table, was half the joy. I was thinking of weather moods that would harmonise with each location.

An early choice was Ardnamurchan, most westerly point of mainland Britain and regarded by sailors out of the Clyde as a sort of poor man's Cape Horn. Here I would paint my force ten extravaganza and delight in the banners of spray driven over a beleaguered lighthouse. In practice, when we got there the lighthouse was mirrored in a flat blue sea and not a leaf was stirring. I painted it that way partly to acknowledge how few are the real certainties in life and partly because a calm would certainly be needed somewhere. My obligatory storm finally caught up with us nearer to the aptly named Cape Wrath.

High on the list from the beginning however, was Chesil Beach and this picture was the result of a bracing day on the Dorset Downs above Abbotsbury, trying to achieve it.

The bank itself and the lake it has formed, the 'Fleet', have always fascinated me as one of our great geomorphological wonders. A pleasing curve of perfectly formed shingle, ten miles long, reaches out to the whale-back hump of Portland, holding back the tumult of Lyme Bay while affording shelter to the Fleet from the worst of the south-westerlies.

Up on the hill above, however, several heavy lumps of chalk were needed to steady the legs of a rickety easel against the constant buffets of the wind.

Chichester Harbour

Oil on board 18" x 24" (1978)

The tidal creek, the mud and the mist was another 'must' for the Shell Calendar of Coastlines. But this time the subject was closer to home.

Half-a-mile round the sea-wall from the cottage where we lived, was Dip Rythe, a natural tidal creek rudely cut off when Napoleonic prisoners-of-war built up the wall and reclaimed the land behind.

Today the drains of the fresh marsh run their surplus water into the creek at low water. The incoming tide closes a flap-valve as the sea rises to the very rim of the bank – and sometimes over the top.

This was a pilgrimage I made almost daily, with my binoculars, for there was always something interesting in the Rythe. So here at last was a subject where I could wait for the exact weather I wanted before venturing from home, then just walk along there carrying my bits and pieces and start painting.

Blue-eyed Shags

Oil on board – sides 28″ (1978)

If nothing else, here is a departure from convention. Rectangular shapes for pictures have always been the norm, even with artists desperate to appear novel. The choice then confines itself to 'portrait' or 'landscape' in format and oddly enough, seldom square. Circular and oval pictures used to happen in the old romantic days but this is the only *square* picture, hung at 45 degrees from the logical, to form a diamond, that I ever saw. The idea came, as many ideas do, in the bath.

I had been busying myself with drawings of shags posing around their breeding ledges. They were the blue-eyed ones of the Antarctic and Sub-Antarctic, and without doubt, the most handsome shags there are.

Because the height of their nesting cliff was crying out for emphasis, I tried it first with an upright rectangle. It was then apparent that this allowed insufficient space for the horizontal tops of the ledges and a more generous sideways spread that was becoming increasingly important.

This must have been the point at which the bath entered the story, bringing with it the realisation that a square shape set on end would offer by its extra length across the corners, just what I needed. I even discovered that the sloping upper edges became strangely suggestive of an overhang to the cliff and added a little something to the character of those vertical bird communities.

There was never an intention to offer painting tips within these pages – it would not be fitting in the light of the scanty artistic training already described. But for what it is worth, I can recommend this shape whole-heartedly, to anyone faced with the need to paint blue-eyed shags standing about on columnar basalt.

Swans through the Baltic

Oil on board 40″ x 60″ (1978)

For me this picture has always enjoyed enduring associations with Slimbridge, the Scott family and the Wildfowl Trust before 'Wetlands' was added to its title.

Everyone was a bit swan-happy in those days – Bewick's swan-happy – painting them, sketching them, writing books and scientific papers about them and delighting in the new discovery that, like human fingerprints, each swan could be recognised individually by the patterns in yellow and black on its bill. Indeed it was the bills of swans that turned my god-daughter Dafila into Dr D. K. Scott!

When the birds arrived in autumn to take over the mere outside Peter's studio window, each one was welcomed in by name, logged and monitored and appropriate names bestowed upon any newly acquired mates.

Swan records were gathered at the fenland centre of Welney too and recognisable swans picked up by 'mug-shots' as well as leg rings on other favourite ports of call on their migration. Teams from Slimbridge would travel to Russia and with unusual co-operation for the cold-war period, pursue their studies of our winter visitors on to the tundras that skirt the Siberian coast from the Kanin Peninsula eastwards to the Lena. This is the wilderness in which they breed.

When they returned, often with cygnets yet to be named, it was surprising how quickly they accepted the lighted room beside their lake and the strange people inside it. When darkness fell we crept about like zombies, Peter intoning 'Hands of a clock – move like the hands of a clock.' No sin could have been more grievous than a thoughtless movement that might spread alarm across swan lake; but the hands of the clock routine, it must be stressed, applied only to visitors. Sudden movements by Scotts were always acceptable to the swans.

On a table in the window lay a little brass telescope that had belonged to the great Northumberland engraver and naturalist Thomas Bewick, – born in 1753. It was engraved with his name and by his own hand, Bewick, who had given his name to the swan. Unwittingly he had left a legacy of delight to future generations – a hallowed look at Bewick's own swans, through Bewick's own telescope – even if the birds were all delicately fringed with the colours of the spectrum.

In the midst of all this swan-happiness, and repressing any urge to jump on the table-top and dance a hornpipe, I thought about the swans on their way through the Baltic to keep their dates with destiny at Slimbridge. A large picture for large birds, I thought – and this was the result. It was 40″ x 60″.

Bryant and May, makers of Swan Vestas matches, hung the picture in the entrance hall of their offices and made prints from it under a scheme that greatly helped the Trust's research work at the time.

We still have one of those prints, hanging on an upstairs landing where I see it often and it continues to evoke the memories I have described. It seems that the Wildfowl and Wetlands Trust, Slimbridge and Bewick's swans in general, are a very special trinity and have jointly bequeathed some indelible and cherished memories.

72

A Pintail Marsh

Oil on board 24" x 36" (c 1979)

One of the famous sporting writers of the late nineteenth century, described the yearly sadness that accompanied the laying up and greasing of his punt-gun. '. . . As I walked back from the boat-house, I became aware that primroses were raising their sickly heads, a big ugly butterfly was jigging about, another spring was at our throats . . .' One must admit that here is a man with the mind made up. There would have been no vacillation from him about which was his favourite time of year.

For the rest of us, I feel the decision is just as difficult to reach as naming our favourite bird, our most beautiful flower, colour, meal, book, picture or anything else. The whole issue is cluttered up with qualifications and this, of course, is what makes any discussion on the subject, such enormous fun.

Comparisons between seasons is a never-ending debate and long may it remain so, because in the process some new viewpoint can be thrown up which alters one's thinking thereafter. Our family is always at it because they are all into gardening and trees and water-tables. Where livelihood is concerned, issues must go beyond simple preferences for looking at and living in, to what has to be done in one season for the next one to achieve its best. A sense of obligation has entered the equation.

I am now trying to get out from under all this having reached the age when conscience will allow the eating of a little lightly-boiled lotus. *And*, I tell myself, I am a painter and must accept the need for wandering about, looking at and trying to 'capture' (lovely expression) things in paint. It is wonderfully harmless and often spiritually rewarding. The result of this attitude is interesting – I still have no idea which is my favourite time of year.

There is one I would not choose and that is the end of a long, overblown and buzzing summer. This always brings a longing for autumn to get on with it. There comes the need for a change of colours, a little less green, and all that lovely 'mellow fruitfulness' bit – red admirals flexing their wings on the ivy flowers in the last of the summer sun. (I suspect that my Victorian sporting writer would also be feeling his oats just now.)

I must apologise for the long preamble before getting to the subject of this painting – a pintail marsh. The month is March. Perhaps everything considered, March *is* my favourite month, both for its winter colours lingering on and its promise of a burgeoning spring around the corner. It is a month to arouse all the most easily understood enjoyments of living.

This is typically a March landscape, up in the Border country of Dumfries and Galloway where our eldest son Jason and his family live. Last summer's reeds still stand, brown and rustling, the marsh is full after winter rains and the sky a procession of boisterous clouds. These March days are all sparkle and move-ment, with a flight of pintails, surely the loveli-est of all ducks, to be the prime movers.

Afternoon in Samburu

Oil on board 24" x 36" (1981)

One of the practical artistic exercises we were encouraged to perform at school was a self-portrait. It was deemed better than painting someone else and for a very sound reason. The logic was that one tended to get bored with painting and bored with sitting still at the same time. The student had total mastery of both inclinations. Of course the resulting portrait was back to front and few people realise quite how asymmetrical a human face can be, but it mattered little to the student because what he saw on the canvas was what the poor fellow saw when he made his cautious attempts at shaving. He knew better than anyone else whether or not a 'likeness' had been achieved.

Models in art schools are professionals. They earn their living by standing, lying or sitting still – often in unusual postures. They endure what must amount to hours of protracted discomfort and presumably without the inner spiritual rewards of a bed of nails. Theirs is a livelihood in which every penny is earned.

These kind of thoughts passed through my mind one afternoon at Samburu in the Northern Frontier District of Kenya. I had never encountered a wild animal that though wide awake, lay so still for so long, with no movement more distracting than the lifting of an eyebrow or a nervous tick which twitched at the last few inches of the tail which for the most part, hung flaccid as a resting bell-rope.

Here indeed was the heaven-sent gift to the artist. The leopard had found a branch formed to perfection for the flexible body of a feline, and put it to full use. Sat in the hatch of the Land-Rover we drew him from below – pages of charcoal drawings. Ever optimistic, I even took the occasional photograph which I have learned from experience to be of little use. Any camera in my hands, from my first Box Brownie, has been riddled with gremlins. As sophistication grew in cameras, so it seemed, grew my own incompetance. Even the makers of those marketed under the claim of 'idiot proof' know little of the extent of photographic idiocy that is still at large out there. Back would come my slides – too dark, too light, fuzzy edged, heads missing, or plain black and wasted because I had forgotten all about the battery!

After a full half-hour our model rose up in slow-motion, gave an apologetic cough, turned like a dead-beat compass needle onto a reciprocal bearing and lowered himself effortlessly down on to the branch again – facing the other way.

Legs now hung in new positions, tail was at the other end and there was a new profile. For another half-an-hour he was to remain static. It was as if some all-powerful art master in the sky had set us a new pose for the next period of instruction and we started in again gratefully, pencils scratching, charcoal smudging until we had worked something out and the period came to an end.

We left the leopard in peace then, bumping off through the acacias towards the track back to camp. There we stopped for a final look back at our model through binoculars. This time his posture was very slightly different. Perhaps it was just that his audience had gone and he was alone again. One last look and it was all explained. This time he was fast asleep.

A Pond in the Woods

Oil on board 14″ x 28″ (1981)

1983 saw another Shell Calendar, this time with the theme 'Freshwater View.' The three subjects that follow were chosen to feature some different forms in which fresh water presents itself. As with the seascapes, one of these water forms was waiting very close to home – just fifty yards away, in Tournebury Woods. It became the subject for January.

No pond was ever formed with greater violence or speed than this one, the deep and circular crater of a bomb intended for Portsmouth, in 1942. Shattered trees lay around it and brackish water soon seeped in. By the time the War ended it was brim-full and mature with the scarring healed, only its circular outline betrayed its origin.

In the years that followed even this became mellowed and obscured by trees that had fallen with more natural grace and subsidence of its steep clay banks. By the winter of 1981, when this picture was painted, it was just another pond in the woods. There were others there already (old clay workings) the last reminders of a thriving brickworks that just survived the turn of the century. Indeed the two-up-two-down cottage where we lived had been built to house the manager of the Tournebury Brickfields.

Heavy snow that year overlay the frozen pond like a table-cloth and carried the tell-tale prints of passers-by in the night. One morning a fox was there first to make his own furtive inspection.

A Bridge in Strathgarve

Oil on board 14″ x 18″ (1981)

Highland river was the choice for a spring month in the Shell Calendar, as the year began to awake. No subject can be more excitingly variable than freely running water: in spate, the colour of peat; between times, clear as gin, and at all times filling the ears with the music of its mood. Any such river would suffice, so the choice became a lottery.

Then we saw this old bridge in Strathgarve. I can never cross a bridge without stopping to lean over and look for trout, or salmon if they are running. Here the bridge itself brought an extra appeal.

These highland bridges have grown there, out of their landscape. Just a few yards away, the evidence of quarrying for the essential stone is still discernable and this imparts a rare integrity to the structure – a feel of 'belonging.' The indigenous granite has simply been rearranged to fulfil a purpose; a by-product of the effort is the provision of a perfect foil to the rough-hewn shapes of the river-bed's natural geology. From down below you could look up and see blue sky under the arch and the whole sweep of it seemed to be as much in flight as the passing oystercatcher.

The colour of the water that day was certainly not peat, nor yet gin, more like a good Islay Malt. It echoed the colours of sun-warmed rock and even, in places, the new green of the burgeoning larch and the oystercatcher's call cut clearly through the background rumble of the falls.

Loch and Mountain – Beinn Dearg

Oil on board 14" x 18" (1981)

This was to be my offering for autumn, in the Shell Calendar. I had painted a frozen pond and a spring river so I needed a lake, but I badly wanted mountains to go with it. As most of this combination lies north of the Tweed (with every respect to the English lakes) my lake was going to be a loch.

Just north of the road from Inverness to Ullapool, lies Loch Glascarnoch – its level maintained by a dam at its eastern end.

Shallow bays stretch like fingers into the lower levels of Dirrie More, leaving smooth beaches of sand and peat, deeply cut here and there by burns from a classic U-shaped glen.

Every so often the whole vista was swept by curtains of sleet, sudden bright clearances followed by snow-flurries that hid everything, only to lift and leave a mantle of white. Two thousand-foot Leacachain is to the left and to the right stands 3,500-foot Beinn Dearg – most northerly of all the real high tops.

Along the rim of the loch were the slots of a very big stag, perhaps on his way from Straithvaich Forest to Fannich. I never saw him, one so seldom does, and this keeps the legend simmering. There are always bigger stags in the mind than on the hoof. So it was from that source that I drew him, thinking the while of Sir Edwin Landseer in a more romantic era, and how he would have rejoiced in the great beast I had begun to think of as 'The Muckle Hart of Beinn Dearg.'

South from New Zealand: Buller's Albatross

Oil on board 24″ x 36″ (1983)

from the permanent collection of the LEIGH
YAWKEY WOODSON ART MUSEUM –
WISCONSIN – USA.

There are 'great' albatrosses and there are
'mollymawks'. The 'greats' are the
'wandering' and the 'royal', majestic
Southern Ocean flyers with a wing span of
eleven feet or more. Mollymawk species are
more numerous, smaller and more varied in
their patterns – and to my mind, the most
dapper of them all is Buller's.

Buller's albatross has a wing span of about
seven feet, a spirited style of flight and displays a
trusting acceptance of small boats and those
aboard, sweeping in to pass a foot or two away as
if wholly aware of the delight they are providing.

They breed on the islands of Snares and
Solander, south from New Zealand, and
though they spread around the ocean at these
latitudes with others of the albatross kind, this
area is undoubtedly their home.

This painting, the result of my first close and
extended encounter with the birds, is now in
the permanent collection of the Leigh Yawkey
Woodson Art Museum at Wausau, Wisconsin.
For me this was a very great honour; the collection is constantly growing as the museum
establishes itself as the centre of wildlife art in
America and maintains close links with nature
in art (Society for Wildlife Art of the Nations)
at Wallsworth Hall in Gloucestershire.

The Royal Bathing Party

Oil on board 24″ x 36″ (1984)

I have never been 'satisfied' with any picture I have painted – nor I suppose, ever will. But there is this 'cloud cuckoo land' one hears about, so there is no harm in hoping and that is why I tend to look upon every new white rectangle that goes on the easel, as *the* masterpiece about to commence. The fact that in practice it never brings home the bacon is no disappointment – it is just clearing the way for the next attempt.

Once in a while though, a picture will happen which gives me delight. The sensation may fall a little short of satisfaction as I would know it, but it is on the way there. The explanation is that it has achieved, to a great extent, what I was setting out to do and what the original subject had inspired. A good example of such a picture is *The Royal Bathing Party*.

It resulted from a day of contentment, on a beach in the Bay of Islands, South Georgia. King penguins from one of the largest colonies on the island, were making their way with all the in-built dignity of their kind, from the inland slopes to the beach. Among them were young birds in their first glory of adult plumage. Gone was the land-locked juvenile fluff that makes them look like great wads of oakum and had earned them the nickname 'Oakum Boys' from generations of sailors. Elegant and fully fledged now, they were all set for a sea-going life and impatient to begin it. This would be their baptism.

Bills tilted high, long scythe-shaped flippers held a little out from their sides, bellies thrust out before them, they processed down the beach, hundreds strong, with all the self-importance of human dignitaries of Church, State or Academia.

When they reached the water's edge a transformation was suddenly upon them. They became, metaphorically, loud, exhibitionist towel-flicking children, exulting in a new-found prowess in a new-found element. Water will often perform this miracle on humans and animals alike.

Every movement here, which I set out to record in line drawings, also has a purpose far more imperative than play. Parents are teaching their young the skills of the hunt, the agility of survival. As the late Dr Roger Tory Peterson used to say, 'They're darned good at being penguins.'

Underwater Crowd Scene, Komodo – 'Fusiliers' and 'Bar Jacks'

Oil on board 18″ x 36″ (1985)

Reproduced as Limited Edition Print, by Mill Pond Press Inc., 1989

With a cubic foot of salt water weighing 64 pounds and the same volume of air practically nothing, everything about such scenes as this is explained.

Aerial ballet by birds, bats, or insects can only be achieved by frenetic expenditure of energy in one form or another, just to maintain the lift. Aerobatics is one constant battle with gravity, but the undersea is a whole new world in more senses than one, with a whole new repertoire of motions to go with it. Movement becomes a choreography of generally streamlined shapes that slide about with speed in close-knit shoals, pass and re-pass in virtual silence, rise up gently and as gently sink down, spin around or hang there motionless, floating in space. Some blaze with colour and iridescence, others are barely discernible.

Sunlight plays games with the angles of their movements and glows in their translucent fins. The enchantment for a diver is to be a part of it all, savouring the dream-like illusions of flight and weightlessness.

With the subjects here so dominant and so numerous it would be less than fair to withhold their names. The big ones in the foreground are 'bar jacks' (*Carangoides ferdau*). The pilchard-like shoals beyond are 'fusiliers' (*Pterocaesio triliniata*).

A View of Tomorrow

Oil on board 18″ x 30″ (1985)

There are strange sensations about this picture and they are apt to linger even after it is explained. The essence of it is that you are standing in today and looking at tomorrow, which is about two miles away. Consider the location and it falls into place.

The immediate foreground with the bizarre outcrops of rock is a precipitous little island belonging to the USA – Little Diomede. The island just across the way is Great Diomede – the USSR (as it was when the picture was painted). In the far distance beyond can be seen Cape Dezhneva, the extreme eastern tip of continental Asia. Between the two islands is the Bering Strait and down the middle of the Strait runs the International Date Line. If it is Tuesday 23 July here on Little Diomede, over the water it is Wednesday 24.

There are very few days in the year when there is such startling visibility, limited only by the very curvature of the earth – it is normally so thick with sea mist the birds are walking. Looking over the shoulder, due east, I could see the Seward Peninsula of Alaska clearly, though it was thirty-five miles away. It was real luck to be there on such a day.

In the 1980s, with the cold war at its height, these islands represented the closest confrontation between east and west. Looking at 'Russia' through our binoculars we imagined the most sophisticated electronic and optical surveillance equipment known to man, directed at the little Esquimo village of some sixty inhabitants at the foot of the cliff. We imagined every movement of our ship, the little *Lindblad Explorer*, being closely monitored and the information relayed on the minute, to Moscow. But even through the most powerful glasses we could see nothing and gave them credit for being masters of concealment as well.

Years later, in 1993 and following *glasnost* I was working in a Russian nuclear-powered ice-breaker, landed on Great Diomede and saw for myself. There was in fact a sand-bagged bunker on the cliff-top, with a little roof over it, housing a pair of ancient binoculars on a tripod and still trained on the village – but nothing more. I took the liberty of moving them round to scan the huge kittiwake colony nesting in the cliffs below my picture of eight years before. As could be expected, they were flying from today into tomorrow and back into today again, simply getting on with the concerns of being a kittiwake on a beautiful day.

Koalas   Estuarine Crocodile   Golden Lion Tamarins

Oil on boards 14″ x 18″ (1985)

These three pictures are linked as a trio so it would not be unreasonable to treat them together. They are part of a set painted for the People's Trust for Endangered Species for the 1987 fund-raising calendar. Their fellow subjects were a leopard, a bald eagle and a family of blue whales.

Working on them as a group brought a feeling of *déja vu*. Each separate subject and I had crossed paths before in different ways and at different times, leaving their own memories – all but the golden lion tamarins which I had never seen before, wild or captive.

As is often my way with pictures, they were painted together. I have never found it easy to stick with one picture from beginning to end with no interruptions more artistically motivated than a break to make a cup of tea or split a few logs. There is always the need to switch horses as it were, to avoid becoming bored by one particular image outstaying its welcome on the easel. In the normal way of things, there might be several half-finished pictures on the go at any one time in the studio.

With this group, the urge to ring the changes was stronger even than usual. They developed in unison from the charcoal stage to completion. There was a certain logic in this. Each subject shared a common threat from forces in the outside world, the size of their portraits was identical (14″ x 18″) and because they were destined to appear together on the cover I felt there should be some harmony between them. This to some extent, was achieved by small similarities and repetitions of colour from a palette common to them all.

As they took their individual turn for attention, each one aroused certain musings from the past. A neighbour of ours, when I was a schoolboy in Australia, kept a tame koala in his garden and I can still remember what a solid armful it was and what a lovable little creature. He would take us to a forest outside Melbourne where koalas were plentiful in the wild and his tame one travelled with us. There was, not surprisingly, a perpetual smell of eucalyptus about this animal and I remember the statistic that a koala will eat well over a pound of gum leaves a day – a lot of leaves.

Smells are powerfully evocative of places and events. Whenever I crush a eucalyptus leaf – which is not an uncommon delight – there is an immediate recall of that school and its sunny playground, the black-board drawings of kangaroos and lyre-birds, the lizards we kept in our lockers, that filthy ink-well ink on the fingers and of course, that little bundle of an animal with its essentially antipodean smell.

Estuarine crocodiles in their endangered context, have problems that would never face a koala. To many, they represent the very antithesis – level-pegging with snakes, sharks and possibly spiders in the dread/hatred stakes. There is even a question of how anybody, unless bereft of their senses, could wish to save them from extinction anyway. Fortunately there is always a champion of the unpopular somewhere – somebody who will respect, admire and even find affection for a master predator.

I have been lucky with estuarine crocodiles in that I have seen many and some of them huge. Reaching over twenty feet, it is the world's biggest reptile. The first I saw were in 1946, in the islands of the Straits Settlements and on Singapore Island itself. I wonder how many remain today. They would swim just off the beach or lie like great fallen tree trunks in the mud of the mangrove swamps. But the sea-going ones were the best – spotlessly clean, their yellow, olive and black undermarkings clearly defined, the battlements along their backs glinting in the sun. When they came ashore they would sprint to the beachhead and vanish into the undergrowth, leaving tracks to show that their bellies had scarcely touched the sand.

Golden lion tamarins were something altogether new to me. Our first meeting was at the London Zoo. Just how much of what I saw was 'zoo behaviour,' I shall never know. I just remember that these were the most twitched-up, frenetic little animals I have ever met. They were never still for an instant. If they ever stopped leaping around it would be to have a scratch, and that so driven by urgency, the hand or foot involved became as blurred as a hummingbird's wing.

They were not the easiest of animals to draw, but occasionally they would freeze for perhaps half a second, affording that fleeting image that finds its way into subliminal advertising. The pencil would scribble a few lines while a charged memory tried to do the rest.

In those frozen-frame stills they offered, it was the eyes that were all-powerful – little round ones like greasy boot-buttons. Their heads were close together, peering from different angles – in duplicate. I began to feel that a little more of this kind of appraisal and I would find myself up in the trees and doing the same.

A Happening at Sea

Oil on board 24″ x 36″ (1985)

The magical mix of courage, hardiness, expertise and the generosity with which they are offered, puts the lifeboat close to the heart of all the nation. There is no need to be a sailor or even live by the sea – admiration is there in the genes. Even the rattled collection box is like meeting a friend and nobody feels embarrassed to be seen rattling it.

Yet it is only when one looks at the listings of 'services' performed around the coasts in an average year, that one begins to understand the scale of this navy of amateur heroes in readiness, round the clock, to offer whatever calls may be made on their skills – for others.

Back in the early eighties, a generous benefactor made it possible for the Royal National Lifeboat Institution (RNLI) to bring its pictorial record of rescues at sea more up to date. Several incidents were listed as a varied cross-section of circumstance and outcome, that could offer possible subjects.

As I remember, there were about five of them, and spread from Caithness to Cornwall, but one immediately caught my eye. It was a rescue off Eastoke Head, Hayling Island on 14 December 1980 – Service No. 1581.

It grabbed me because I knew the people, the place, the sea conditions and remembered the extent of local pride at the outcome. This picture was the result of my attempt, on the RNLI's behalf, to reconstruct this happening at sea.

RNLI reports, together with coastguard information, are detailed and fascinating. Everything is there in black and white and includes any relevant testimony that may come in from other witnesses, ashore and afloat. Reading this one through was enough to begin sketching out all the relative positions of the players in the drama – an arrow for the wind's direction and a figure for its strength. The imagination then, was filling in the way such a wind would have moulded the shapes of waves and the extent of their malevolence over the very familiar Hayling Bar.

The casualty was a 7-metre 'Sonata' Class yacht with four aboard. Her rudder had been carried away, leaving her helpless off a lee shore in a force 8 south-westerly gale. Her crew had done all they could do, fired their red flares – and hoped the anchor would hold.

A 'Wessex' V helicopter from HMS *Daedalus* at Lee-on-Solent stood by but was unable to use the winch for the wild girations of the yacht's mast as she wallowed in a beam sea. It was able though, to guide the Hayling Lifeboat, an Atlantic 21 rigid inflatable, out to the scene and remain there in case things got worse.

The haste with which the lifeboat had to be launched was a critical factor and stood on no ceremony. The first to arrive on the scene became the crew and were immediately away – Frank Dunster, Trevor Pearce, shore helper and first aider, and Graham Wickham, aged 16 and normally a launcher. Frank Dunster took the helm.

There were survival problems enough just getting there, followed by four or five passes to come alongside and snatch off whom they could on each attempt. At last all four were safely aboard the lifeboat, including one whose agility was somewhat hampered by a metal leg. Trevor Pearce had broken a knee in the process and Dunster had damaged a hand.

They all received commendations for a courageous service successfully concluded 'Service No. 1581.' Frank Dunster was awarded the Institution's Bronze Medal.

The Cottage from the Creek

Oil on board 12" x 18" (1987)

This is a demure little picture but it represents something very special in the lives of our family. It was 'home' for 35 years and a great many of the pictures in this book, though often of far-away subjects, were painted here.

When we began to outgrow the place with a buregeoning family, I acquired a wooden shed that had been designed as a produce stall for a market garden and by substituting glass for roof-shingles on the north-facing slope, reinvented it as a studio.

The 'studio', as might have been expected, became the butt of much humour. The description was perhaps a little pretentious, especially as its use alternated with the name used in the supplier's catalogue – 'The Improved ASTORIA produce stall (£250 delivered and erected on site).' This in turn became corrupted by a disrespectful family, to 'The Hermitage' because it was here that the 'hermit,' as he was sometimes called, went to hide out of earshot of the cottage, to paint his pictures or to sulk.

Inevitably it became ever more cluttered with boat gear, overflow bunks, chain saws and tins of diesel fuel, to an extent where my parents' predictions of an artist's penurious decline amid ever-increasing squalour, began to assume a disturbing reality.

The day this picture was painted, my wife and a friend were also painting out on the sea-wall, but facing the other way, concentrating on low-tide mud and the little boatyard across the creek. It was unusual to see such an outburst of creative activity and I began to wonder if a mini version of Mr Finney's Newlyn Art Group was about to take root here on Chichester Harbour.

Strangely this is one of very few I painted of the cottage itself, despite my love of the place. The woods behind, the creeks, the fresh marsh inside the sea-wall, boats stranded on mud or riding to moorings at high water; these were the ever-present and beckoning subjects.

Not infrequently, the biggest spring tides, bolstered by a south-west gale, would breach the sea defences and we would have spectacular floods. I even had fantasies of the ASTORIA produce stall, transformed into a latter-day Ark, floating serenely away, hermit at the helm, to ground after the prescribed period, on some remote and romantic Ararat along the South Downs.

Floods and changing seasons brought birds to the door – shelducks courting in spring on the rabbit-nibbled lawn, brent geese in their hundreds, their clamour filling the night as well as the day.

Autumn and spring migrations brought wader hoards to the mudflats and the outer sands and to the marshes next to the house. Small passage birds came, pied flycatchers and redstarts, to linger a day or two before moving on. They never nested with us.

A passage I found in *Wake* (Author Keith Shackleton, 1954, Lutterworth Press) fairly describes the family lifestyle over those 35 years.

'Above all, the cottage is a place that is tied up with the sailing of small boats, and cluttered up with their gear; the hours of its inhabitants are controlled by the height of the barometer and the state of the tide; we are dry when we leave it in the morning and soaked when we return. The warming fires are of driftwood, burning with the mellow light imparted by salt, and the occasional flicker of green where an unseen copper rivet has left its influence on the flames.'

Inevitably the idyll came to an end. The famous 'October Hurricane' of 1987, the year this picture was painted, tracked on to the island with clinical accuracy. It took us two days to clear the track through; the glorious woods were devastated. Though the cottage itself stood unscathed, the produce stall of the endearing names, was flattened by a falling macrocarpa tree and the northern foreshore of Chichester Harbour became a panorama of maritime mayhem.

The whole scene, the whole ambience, had changed overnight and we came to see it as a signal. We were being told that the time was near for moving on.

After sorting things out as best we could, we headed west two years later. A long chapter that from the very start, had brimmed over with gratitude to the owners who had welcomed us, and included excitement, fulfilment, simple nautical joys and the call of curlews, had come to an end.

Keith Shackleton 87

Motu Iti, Motu Nui, Motu Kao Kao and *Sea Cloud* – Easter Island

Oil on board 12″ x 15″ (1987)

Suddenly confronted with this picture again, after a gap of ten years, my first impulse was to rummage through the shelves for a copy of the log I had kept during the voyage concerned. Much of it I found was not just relevant to this little picture of a tall ship in the Pacific, but to this book as a whole. Here are some extracts which throw light on the writer's aims and beliefs at the time – as well as rekindling happy personal memories.

Maiden South Pacific Voyage
SY *Sea Cloud*

Preface

Logbook notes are very personal things. They are a rag-bag of facts, happenings, conjecture, philosophy and sometimes nonsense. Often they contain drawings and there is certainly one consistent factor here – they are never as good as their author would wish.

In no way can a logbook cover everything, any more than it can avoid demonstrating the writer's bias of interests. So, I offer these, the log of the voyage of SY *Sea Cloud* from Easter Island to Tahiti – April 1987.

An alternative would be to have logbooks compiled by a committee, but if this frightening concept ever came to pass, I feel you would not have been able to read thus far by this date . . .

Thursday 9 April 1987

. . . On the seaward side where the land falls away in precipitous cliffs, was enacted the ceremony of the Birdman. Much of it is told in the rock carvings here – the election of new nobility by contestants swimming to the offshore skerries of Motu Iti and Motu Nui to bring back the first egg of the sooty tern. Today the sooty terns are as extinct as the participants. A few chimango caracaras – the carrion hawks of southern South America – patrol the headland and are credited with the loss of the seabirds; an accusation which I believe contains more fancy than fact.

On the very tip of the sail-like rock Motu Kao Kao, a pair of boobies stood like bookends facing east and west. While we watched, our home for the next three weeks, *Sea Cloud*, cruised outside the breakers and turned back to Hanga Roa in search of a more comfortable anchorage.

Later in the voyage there comes an entry which continues the voyage westwards and adds a little more background to the ship that looks so tiny in the picture.

Bounty Bay, Pitcairn Islands

17 April – Good Friday

I believe the lasting memory will be the warmth of the welcome, the spectacle of naturally acquired competence and seamanship, cooperation and camraderie, so typical of island people and isolated communities.

Their faith seemed to be their strongest single bond and when they left us, the two longboats pulling away into the dusk, they sang hymns of farewell. Voices well practised in perfect harmony . . . 'the beautiful, the beautiful river' came over the water as one voice – and from people to whom a river of any kind can have existed only in the mind.

Nobody aboard *Sea Cloud* will readily forget Pitcairn. Nor I think, will the islanders forget this elegant square-rigged ship, so close to all their inborn concepts of the sea.

Ten years on there is even a short postscript. My younger son Jasper met Joanna, the sailmaker aboard *Sea Cloud* – at Easter Island. They are now married and their little motorcar is called 'Motu Nui.'

Frigatebirds, Flying Fish and Mahi Mahi

Oil on board 24" x 36" (1987)

It had been a long voyage in the square-rigger *Sea Cloud*, through the South Pacific from Easter Island to Tahiti, via a host of islands and most of it under sail. Each day provided some new and special wonder as is the way with the sea.

In the Marquesas we had watched the most graphic illustration of the food chain at work I have ever seen. It began with small seabirds (terns and petrels) hunting minute and closely-packed surface fish, themselves hotly pursued by shoaling, mackerel-sized predators. These in turn were under attack from diving boobys above and tuna from below. Joining the chase were fish of increasing size, enormous wahoo and the occasional spearfish. Dolphins were also leaping and rolling in the mêlée and at the very back, serene and purposeful, came a pod of sperm whales, lunge-feeding at the surface. Here was the ultimate feeding frenzy – everything according to size, cashing in on this sudden gesture of bounty from the ocean.

Awesome as it was and unforgettable, it inspired no picture. But a later encounter on the same voyage was more contained, more organised and pictorially, altogether more welcoming. Moreover it was a happening that text books dwell upon and few things come more satisfying than seeing the real enactment of a familiar verbal description.

Frigatebirds, already seen at their courtship ceremonial, are unique among sea birds in their lack of effective waterproofing. Though they travel large distances at sea, they always return to roost ashore, having kept their plumage dry through every feeding manouvvre of the day. Masters of aerobatics, they will force a booby to disgorge in flight, then dropping below, will snatch up the jettisoned fish before it reaches the water.

Their favourite diet of all, however, are flying fish – already the first choice of the swift-swimming mahi mahi, or dolphin fish. Hounded from below, the flying fish take to wing – only to be met by the other half of a formidable, though entirely opportunist, hunting partnership.

The sight of this everyday practice close alongside, rung all the bells needed. Many find the picture sinister, with the birds striking a note of dark foreboding. But it has to be remembered that frigatebirds, along with certain other maligned creatures, are simply conducting their lives as nature intended. For me it was a subject too graphic and too sensational to miss.

Bald Eagle over the LeConte Glacier – Alaska

Oil on board 24" x 30" (1987)

The LeConte is the southernmost tide-water glacier in North America. Ice garnered from the 10,000-foot Kate's Needle, the 9,000-foot Devil's Thumb, Castle Mountain and Twin Peaks (both over 7,000 feet) is finally deposited into the sea at the head of Frederick Sound.

Like most Alaskan glaciers it is steep and fast flowing, calving constantly and filling LeConte Bay with a jumbled assortment of ice shapes from the size of a fist to the size of a house.

This was another very special place shared with my friend Franz Lazi, the film-maker from Stuttgart. Secured in the back of a Beaver floatplane with the door removed, he was having the time of his life, recording it all from the glacier's foot to its birth place below the peaks. I was free just to look and make occasional scribbled notes of a maze of crevasses and the lofty séracs that leaped from their depths towards the little plane. Then came a slice of real fulfilment when a single bald eagle, untroubled by our presence, slid below us, its background surreal in every aspect – but at the same time, the purest manifestation of nature, and fashioned from ice alone.

'Flying' through Kelp – King Penguins

Oil on board 24″ x 36″ (1988)

Penguins, along with the dodo and others, have become an accepted symbol of flightlessness. Even in the RAF the word has been used in a slightly derogatory way to denote the grounded.

However, there is no logical reason why flight should be seen as exclusive to passage through air. Aerodynamics and hydrodynamics share identical principles – all that differs is the relative density of medium. The penguin's flipper is a perfect aerofoil shape but its reduced area is designed to perfection for flight under the sea. Any scuba diver will confirm how close all this comes to the illusion of self-propelled flight that features in some of the more enjoyable types of dreams.

Poetry of motion is a fair description of the penguin's underwater life-style. With the leisurely laid-back wing beat one associates with a heron, they speed through the water like the passage of a torpedo. After a dive from the surface, they bring down trapped air to be shed like silver sequins and linger in their wake.

Their background here, is the ubiquitous kelp, fathoms of it, honey-brown against the blue-green of depth. It hangs in languid, sensuous curves and by passing through its stationary curtain and leaving obstacles behind, the penguins give an impression of doubling their speed.

Keith Shackleton 88 ©

Hourglass Dolphins

Oil on board 18″ x 36″ (1988)

There is a clear comparison between this picture and the last. Both are of swift creatures under water, shaped for the element and in the kind of transient activity that once witnessed, is never forgotten and cries out to be painted. And it has to be, for until it is there is no peace of mind or relaxation.

I have had the luck to swim with dolphins several times and in widely different places – once even to play with a pod of six, along with some of my shipmates, off a Falklands beach. Those were the fat little half-black-half-white ones – Commerson's dolphins, known as 'puffing pigs' in the Islands. They had joined the first Zodiac from the ship as close escort, when we went in to check out the landing.

They played in the shallows, swimming between our legs and thumping against our knees. All that day my Zodiac was a bath-toy to them and when it was finally lifted aboard on the crane, I looked down and saw them treading water below, bodies half out of the water, begging it seemed, to have their ball back. Anthropomorphism again: it is a temptation hard to avoid when an animal of such obvious 'intelligence' is reaching out for contact and company.

The species in the picture however, are hourglass, or Cruciger dolphins and I must admit to choosing them in preference to the puffing pigs only because, pictorially, they offered a more promising pattern. Perhaps they qualify as another of these 'designer' animals – the hourglass motif carried like 'go-faster' stripes on a smart new aeroplane.

The real excitement with dolphins under the sea is to witness the reverse of the normal, to see one leap upward from sight then return to view at a steep angle, with a flash of captive light. Like the penguins, he too is coated momentarily in silver before losing himself again in the kinetic throng.

Gale in the Coral Sea – *Elizabeth Bligh*

Oil on board 12″ x 18″ (1989)

At sunrise, on 28 April 1789, William Bligh, Captain of HMS *Bounty*, with eighteen loyal crew, was cast adrift by Fletcher Christian and his fellow mutineers. They were thirty miles off the island of Tofua, in what Cook had called 'The Friendly Islands' – the Tonga Group.

There followed the longest open-boat voyage and one of the most brilliant epics of seamanship in history – 3,600 nautical miles to Timor (now Indonesia) from whence a passage home could be assured.

While working on the tall ship *Sea Cloud* in the Pacific nearly 200 years later, our younger son Jasper, noticed the approaching bicentenary and resolved on the instant to build an exact replica of *Bounty's* launch, somehow get her out to Tonga by the appropriate date, and as a tribute to one of the most maligned men who ever went to sea, sail Bligh's course again.

A small group of us got together and formed the William Bligh Trust, to raise funds and support for the final endeavour under the title 'In the Wake of William Bligh.' Here two names stand out in special gratitude, for enthusiasm, encouragement and help of every kind – Sir John Smith and the late Capt. John Wells RN.

No sooner back from the Pacific, Jasper went down to the National Maritime Museum at Greenwich, to borrow shipwrights' drawings of the launch. Through the co-operation of the Maritime Trust, he was able to build her in their workshops at Gosport. She was launched, christened and ready for sailing trials, in July 1988.

Elizabeth Bligh, named for Bligh's wife, completed a few gruelling voyages in the Channel, in the belief that such knobbly areas as the Portland Race would condition her crew for anything that might be expected from the benign trade winds of the Pacific. (A little irony was to creep in later.)

The Bank Line – one of the earliest supporters – agreed to ship her, deck-cargo, at least as far as Samoa, together with her crew and stores; more generous offerings came from victuallers and yacht chandlers at home.

At daybreak again, on 28 April 1989, Jasper Shackleton and his crew, James Armstrong, a fireman at London Airport, Ian Lawson, a Doctor from Stornoway, Angus McCallum a Chartered Accountant and Robin Todd (an itinerant Yacht Master of 'no fixed abode'), set sail from the exact co-ordinates off Tufua, 200 years to the very hour, after William Bligh.

'Lizzy' as they knew her, was much better equipped and much more lightly laden. They carried safety gear and radio, desalination equipment, modern clothing and food, fishing gear, a shotgun and a keg of Pusser's Rum. Purist ethics however, forbade any state-of-the-art navigational aids and they relied on Bligh's methods. But at least they had charts, he had been forced to rely on memory from past voyages and four cutlasses for protection. They even stole his watch. Clearly Bligh was never expected to survive.

At home we had studied all the manuals. The longest leg was the stage from Port Vila, Vanuatu, across the Coral Sea to the Great Barrier Reef off Queensland. The manual proclaimed a steady force three from the south-east, a breeze made-to-measure, and that it held for this whole period. Bligh had experienced just this and on a comfortable broad reach he crossed in under two weeks, overloaded as he was.

As events turned out for his followers however, the ensuing 200 years had seen the arrival of Murphy's Law. Three days into the Coral Sea, about 60 miles off New Caledonia, the wind headed them, went round to the west and began to blow up to force nine and the gale held for 36 hours. They sat it out riding to a sea anchor rigged from the stern, which offered better buoyancy to face the weather and better rudder control. They settled down like this, denied their brew-up of tea or a change of clothing until the gale abated and the wayward elements had decided it was time to obey the words of the manual.

Because they had been forced so far to the east and for so long, it took altogether 23 days to reach 'Bligh Boat Passage' through the Great Barrier Reef, into Australian coastal waters. There were a lot of worried people at home – their radio had packed up even before Vanuatu.

The remainder of the voyage was pleasantly uneventful, up the Queensland coast to Thursday Island and across the Arafura Sea to Kupang, Timor – another two weeks making six in all. That had been about Bligh's time too, but he was unable to stop because of cannibals. Two hundred years on there was an altogether friendlier welcome.

There is however, a sequel to relate. When Bligh reached Kupang, East Indiamen were loading and discharging in the harbour. The Navy was there. The port was a bustling staging post for Far Eastern commerce.

Two hundred years later it is something entirely different. After six weeks in an open boat, the 'authorities' denied them a landing because Kupang is not an 'Official Port of Entry.' They were forced to sail on another 500 miles to Bali where a generous-spirited administration allowed a 'ship' to enter. Thus Bligh's open-boat record of 3,600 miles had been exceeded – and for the most ludicrous of reasons.

It should go without saying, that my picture of *Elizabeth Bligh* riding to her drogue in a force nine, is from imagination alone – prompted by descriptions from her stalwart crew.

Gyrfalcon at Home

Oil on board 24" x 36" (1989)

Published as Limited Edition Print by Mill Pond Press Inc., Florida, 1989

This glacier was a classic, snaking down from the ice-cap miles to the north, scouring the valley floor with its relentless progress, finally dumping its burden of ice into the fjord below. Every term of glaciology was demonstrated here as if a writer of handbooks had designed a landscape to illustrate *'bergschrund'* and *'fernline'*, *'median'* and *'marginal moraine'*, *'crevasse'* and *'sérak'*. Where its snout reached salt water, it calved off into *'brash-ice'*, *'bergy-bits'* and the occasional monster consequential enough to be called *'iceberg.'*

Scrambling up to the viewpoint was a joy in itself, firm holds for hands and feet, burgeoning alpine plants, but birds in meagre measure, the occasional Lapland longspur, a wheatear and a few snow buntings – then a single ptarmigan. It was windless and silent except for those mountain sounds that seem to make silence and solitude the more profound – the rumble of a distant ice-fall and the plaintive cry of a loon.

Sights like this abound in many parts of the Arctic where the landscape thrusts upwards rather than running endlessly on in tundra and distance towards a shallow sea. This particular one is Skoldungenfjord, in southern Greenland.

Sketching it all in the presumptious way artists have, of expecting to distill miles of unsullied wilderness and magnificence into the size of a picture postcard, I was pondering how good it would be to have a gyrfalcon come and sit on the only possible rock. I knew one did from time to time, because I had passed the rock on the way up, picked up an unmistakeable white barred feather and in my fingers, crumbled pellets disgorged by a big falcon – whitened bones, feathers and fur.

Then it came. One seldom sees this really white form, more often they are in variations of speckled, gunmetal grey. It came quite suddenly, strikingly white like some visiting angel and exactly on cue, just as I was packing my rucksack for the scramble back down.

It stayed there for perhaps a minute, no more, but long enough to fix an idea as well as a joyful memory, indelibly in the mind.

Sea-mist, Icebergs and Fulmars – Cape Farewell

Oil on board 24″ x 48″ (1990)

Cape Farewell is to Greenland much as Cape Horn is to South America. It is not just the southernmost point but an island as well, and an island that rises from a system of deep and complicated channels.

My notes for 14 August 1988 record heading into Prins Christian Sund to 'cut off the corner' just as one might head into the Straits of Magellan for the same purpose.

Then, on the evening of that day, this picture presented itself in its stunning reality. The note went on to say that I had made drawings of it and ended with a heavily underlined passage, '*must paint this on return.*'

The little MS *Polaris* emerged from the fjords at a small island called Nunarssuaq, with Cape Farewell itself down to the south-east.

A thick, well-defined stratum of mist about deck-height, lay across the whole scene. The sea was calm and wherever one looked there were fulmars chasing their reflections. But it was the ice monoliths that caught me by surprise. Many huge bergs gather around this southern tip from both sides of Greenland, calved from the great glaciers further north and brought down by the Arctic current and in from the Davis Strait by a counter-flow.

Some of them become grounded here, allowing wave action to wash and reshape their lower contours like half-sucked peppermints the size of a church. Those in the immediate foreground were in shade – but those beyond, where the sun had cleared the mist layer, were flood-lit along their summits in a blaze of colour.

Happenings like this are often short-lived. By the time we had turned to head westwards up the coast, the whole picture had dissolved and was overlaid by a cold, thick duvet of fog.

On the bridge, exclamations of wonderment had all been spent, the radar once more, had become the focus of attention.

Trawlers Fitting-out – Jakobshavn

Oil on board 24" x 36" (1990)

The town's proper Greenlandic name is *Ilulissat* (the Mountains of Ice) but it will take time for charts and popular usage, especially among the aged, to catch up. So the old name survives, *Jakobshavn*.

Like so many other towns it seems to have doubled its size in the last decade. Squeezing into the harbour, let alone the jetties calls for patience and guile. In an effort to relieve congestion, a new flat standing area has been cut out of the mountain to provide space for trawlers to re-fit. They are lifted from the water on a huge gantry and transported across to stand on their own sheer legs, neat and upright for the work to begin.

There are few boats whose lines are not as pleasing as they are functional, especially on dry land where their whole underwater sections are revealed to the eye. Boats are all shapes and sizes but a curve is a curve – it is hard to choose in aesthetic terms, between a thoroughbred racing yacht, a working trawler or even a derelict, discarded on the shore. The in-built integrity of a boat's purpose in life persists into almost complete dilapidation, retaining to the end a form of indestructible beauty.

Be that as it may, the appeal of this subject to me was simply one of contrasts. The hull shapes of these boats were enhanced by the low viewpoint from a Zodiac adrift in the harbour below. They stood in there, each as curvy as a Venus and made to look the more so by a row of parallel piles and the wild confusion of quarried rock.

Blue is also my favourite colour – especially when seen against the warm ochre of the newly formed cliff. I have noticed that blue is also popular with Greenland trawler owners, but was told by a cynic that this was due to the paint supplier's large and advantageously acquired stockholding, rather than deeply felt considerations of art.

Rainbow in the Bow-wave – Antarctic Petrel

Oil on board 24″ x 30″ (1991)

I could never describe myself as 'musical' because I know nothing of the wonders of music's creation nor yet of the means by which it is relayed to appreciative ears. For all that, there have been many occasions when the emotional background brought about by music, has made a profound effect and I believe this beneficent amalgam of love and ignorance is shared by a large proportion of mankind.

Various forms of classical music work this way for me, presumably because they mesh sympathetically with my subliminal thoughts of the moment and the scene I happen to be watching.

Music can work wonders as a quiet background in the studio, like a discreet intravenous injection of encouragement. At other times music has provided accompaniment for a living spectacle, making it almost unbearably moving and in this way, pushed it to the forefront as a subject for another picture.

One I recall, was up on the Ribble Estuary, when wild geese were flying low into a howling blizzard and barely stemming the gale. Despite their exertions, progress was little more than marking time over the house where I was staying.

From an upstairs window, loud and clear, came Haydn's *Concerto for Trumpet and Orchestra*, by courtesy of my host's state-of-the-art radiogram. The mood, the sound, the swirling snowflakes, the shadowy, battling forms of the birds with their own added clamour all came together in one glorious and heroic harmony. I shall never forget it and see it again and again whenever that particular piece is played. I wonder if Haydn had ever watched pinkfeet?

This picture however, concerns a single Antarctic petrel. Music was involved too, and the music was Tchaikovsky's *Swan Lake*.

The alchemy of this experience got away to a good beginning because the solo star was a bird very close to my heart. Antarctic petrels have 'style', achieved by a blend of lovely markings, aerodynamic perfection of shape and a manner of flying that is both graceful and exuberant. Not only are they favourites for visual reasons, they are enigmatic little creatures, unpredictable in their movements. On some voyages they are everywhere, on others they are either absent altogether, or confine themselves to very occasional sightings.

On this day I was leaning over the bridge wing, watching the curl of the bow-wave and the flare of a fleeting rainbow that would appear momentarily in its banner of spray.

Back in the bridge, *Swan Lake* was playing – and loudly enough to hold its own with the wind. Suddenly, and exactly on cue, an Antarctic petrel appeared from nowhere and I had eyes for nothing else. There followed a performance of natural choreography so perfect it seemed the bird herself was receiving the music's pace and moving with it. She kept to the centre stage the bow-wave offered with wild and extravagant twists and turns while the rainbow flickered behind her.

Thus she danced until the tape was switched. Then, as if feeling out of kilter with the music that followed, banked steeply away and sped off over the ocean to dance elsewhere.

Avocets

Oil on board 18″ x 24″ (1991)

There is a curious bird here, with a bill for all the world like a cobbler's awl.' These words, now immortal in our family, were uttered by an octogenarian lady of whom we were all very fond and who now, sadly, is no longer with us. Though deeply sympathetic towards birds in general she never made a study of them. She just constantly asked their names and then forgot the answer.

We were out together that day, on a narrow isthmus on an island in Chichester Harbour. She was passionately fond of going anywhere by boat. She was looking eastward on to a small lagoon. I was looking west over the beguiling area known as Stocker Sands. She was not even carrying binoculars because she claimed they 'distorted things so' and anyway was blessed with eyes as keen as a falcon. But she had immediately noticed the bill, remarked on its unique shape and left no possible doubt as to what she had found.

Until that day I had never seen an avocet and the excitement cannot be overstated. Moreover the bird was only thirty yards away and there were two others with it, scything about among the spartina grass in the shallows.

My delight proved infectious and she shared in the pleasure of having been so closely involved in what was clearly, to me anyway, a special occasion. 'Avocet' thereafter, became one of the few birds names she never forgot, nor did she cease to remind us of the experience.

Fleet of the British Steel Challenge, 1992

Oil on board 24" x 36" (1992)

This event was something of a milestone in ocean racing. It was Chay Blyth's idea, organised by him and billed 'the toughest yacht race ever.'

Ten identical boats were built, using British steel, by DML at Devonport. Sixty-seven feet overall and each sailed by a crew of twelve. The course was round the world, against its rotation, against prevailing winds and ocean currents a total of 28,000 nautical miles.

Each boat was sponsored by a different company so there were ten different colour schemes afloat on their topsides and sails, this being the only aspect in which individual expression was permitted by the inflexible one-design rule.

This scene of them all sailing up the Channel as a fleet was my own personal fantasy. They never did this, but it seemed the best way to display all their spinnakers set together and try to convey an impression of all the thought and detailed planning that lay behind the race.

Initially I painted all the spinnakers as plain white ones, to establish for my own guidance the fall of light and the arrangement of the

boats in the picture. I was already beginning to get cold feet about the company logos and all that lettering which was never my 'thing', but a wife will always step into the breach when she sees a husband's courage on the ebb. I was simply urged to go for it – to paint just one spinnaker each day as a little set task. By Thursday week, she announced encouragingly, they would be finished. Indeed they were. Visualising each logo in a way that conformed to the voluptious contours of the sail proved a rewarding mental exercise.

Group 4 at Cape Horn, 2 December 1992

Oil on board 24″ x 36″ (1993)

Group 4 was one of the contestants in the British Steel round the world race and was involved in a finish so close it could have gone either way up to the last moment. In the event she lost out to *Nuclear Electric*.

These may seem hardly the most romantic names for yachts but their purpose calls for neither explanation nor excuse. They were sailing for the honour and prestige of the companies that sponsored them and in the process, providing experiences of a lifetime for their crews in the best training arena for self-confidence, collective responsibility and a risk of lifelong addiction to the sea. The race proved to be a shot in the arm from industry for a maritime nation.

I was asked to paint *Group 4* at some strategic point in her 28,000-mile voyage. It took only a moment to choose the leg from Rio to Hobart, because this one included the rounding of Cape Horn.

To mariners over the centuries, Cape Horn has to be the most evocative point on the charts. Here the Pacific meets the Atlantic. Boisterous to gale-force westerlies are blowing day in and day out, driving along the west wind drift to speeds of several knots. To round the Horn westabout a vessel must fight both wind and current, close-hauled – and many have succumbed.

William Bligh in the *Bounty* had to give up altogether and run round the world eastwards to make good his landfall in Tahiti. In the great days of sail, the Lutine bell at Lloyds rang for many fine ships, lost without trace or smashed on the rocks of southern Chile. Others, battered and dismasted, limped downwind to the shelter of the Falklands and ended their days as storage hulks.

But fate was smiling on *Group 4*, Mike Golding and his crew. As they stood down the coast of Tierra del Fuego, the wind went round to the east in a miraculous break with tradition. They sped through the Drake Passage south of the Horn on a broad reach, rolling in a confused sea but running fast into the Pacific. It was only then that the westerlies resumed and the Cape was back to its normal, awesome routine.

Before reaching Hobart, Mike Golding sent his report back to England and it was passed on to me. He had given details of the wind speed and direction and the exact sails he had set to take advantage of such a fortuitous turn of events at just the right time and place.

Group 4's story however does not end quite yet. The following year Mike Golding took her to sea again – this time alone. It was an attempt to break Chay Blyth's time of 292 days for a single-handed, non-stop voyage westabout around the world. That was made in 1971 in the Robert Clarke-designed ketch *British Steel*, of 59 feet overall. The achievement stood unchallenged for 22 years. The laurels have now passed to Mike Golding, but Cape Horn, when he reached it a second time, had made all the concessions it was prepared to offer.

Finally, in 1997 this race was sailed once more. Organised again by Chay Blyth (now *Sir* Chay) and the mantle of British Steel taken over by British Telecom. This time *Group 4*, skippered by Mike Golding on the third circumnavigation, was first boat back to Southampton – and winner of the whole race.

North Pole Icescape

Oil on board 14″ x 18″ (1992)

23 August 1992 NORTH POLE

'Today was the attainment of our goal – a goal it must be said, for which many have striven and perished in the attempt, for which spurious claims have been made and accepted without substantiation. It is a point on the map which has never failed to kindle the imagination. In the event we came upon an icescape of pristine beauty (like every other icescape in the Arctic Ocean) – and only the precision of navigational expertise could identify it exactly and lay this ship across the axis of the world. Checking and double-checking took time in heavy ice, crossing and re-crossing, circling, backing and manoeuvring. Finally at 0830 this morning, a Champagne toast was drunk on the bridge, the siren sounded; Captain Anatoly Gorshkovsky was happy with his position.'

An extract from the logbook of the nuclear-powered ice-breaker *Sovetskiy Soyuz*, Trans-Polar Expedition August/September, 1992. Compiled by Keith Shackleton.

I believe the whole ship's company shared the Captain's happiness, but at the same time, the comfort and the capabilities of this magnificent vessel raised small feelings of guilt over all those indomitable folk who had battled here the hard way. In the afternoon I walked out onto the ice and made a little sketch – of which this picture is the result.

Later I noticed that the ship's manoeuvring to maintain her position at 90° North, had opened a few acres of sea around her and an idea suddenly dawned.

The world's oldest Zodiac driver, Founder Member and Admiral of the exclusive Southern Ocean Drivers Society (SODS) would attempt the first ever, single-handed circumnavigation of the globe – by Zodiac. I jumped into my boat and set forth on a glassy sea, completing my circumnavigation in three minutes and 42 seconds.

With a serious eye to competitive record-breaking – and in deference to Chay Blyth – I made a second circumnavigation, this time against prevailing winds, currents and the earth's rotation, the *hard* way. I have to say it took nearly nine seconds longer.

My triumphal homecoming was greeted with a spontaneous and very moving display of applause and congratulation, the sounding of the ship's siren and the presentation of a bottle of vodka by courtesy of the Captain.

In the Ice-breaker's Wake – Sabine's Gulls

Oil on board 24" x 30" (1993)

One of the loveliest things about being north of the Arctic Circle in summer, is the blinding low sun across the sea ice – at midnight. It alchemises every scene and polarises its contents into the brightest light and the darkest shadow.

The place was Amundsen Gulf, between Canada's northern mainland and Victoria Island; here Sabine's gulls breed and are plentiful throughout the summer. Like all gull kind, they have their eyes on the main chance and a working ice-breaker offers one of the best. (I have always believed that when the human race finally packs it in, gulls will take over the world.)

The ice-breaker, whose wake was so rewarding to the gulls and so inspirational to me, was the Canadian coastguard vessel *Camsel*, on her way from Resolute Bay to aid shipping in the Mackenzie.

The low sun threw her shadow endlessly across the ice as she beavered away, leaving a deep ice canyon and open water astern. All the while her thrashing propeller was turning up marine goodies of every description, augmented by scraps from the galley, and the gulls were taking their harvest.

The whole spectacle appealed because it combined intense movement with striking contrasts of light and dark. The jostling birds deep in the wake, became deep in colour too. Directly they lifted out of shadow they exploded into light again.

This is something I have watched often with dolphins under a ship's bow, where their underwater colours show greens and blues. As they leap into sunlight, their warm bronze and honey-coloured flanks are momentarily revealed, survive the aerial leap and return immediately to the tones and colours of the undersea. This was the first time I had watched the same uplifting phenomenon, with birds.

'Driftwoodscape' with Ross's Gulls

Oil on board 18″ x 24″ (1993)

This is as improbable a place as one can imagine. The River Lena rises in eastern Siberia not far from Lake Baykal and flows some 1200 miles north to the Laptev Sea and the Arctic Ocean. It winds through densely forested and quite hilly country which, north of the tree-line, flattens out into tundra and finally forms what must be one of the world's biggest deltas, covering 15,000 square miles, well to the north of the Arctic Circle.

Like all deltas, the Lena is a maze of channels, some deep and navigable, others shallow, wide and tortuous. On the flat, alluvial ground between, lies a seemingly endless natural phenomenon which I can only describe as a 'driftwoodscape'.

With the break-up of the ice each year, for millennia floods along the Lena have brought down roots and whole trees in their millions and spread them over the flats. So here lie ancient, overgrown stumps of sub-fossil antiquity overlayed by freshly uprooted trees weathered only by last spring's thumping down rapids far upstream.

Here at last I saw Ross's gull, the rare and arcane little northern bird with its curious and unexplained movements all around the Arctic and haphazard wanderings to places further south. This is an area where they breed, the young of the year are around and like so many birds in these sort of places, very tame.

You might well ask how anyone finds their way into the middle of the Lena delta to paint Ross's gulls and the answer is mundane – by helicopter from the Russian ice-breaker working off-shore. It is an odd feeling of both privilege and loneliness when the noisy thing clatters off into oblivion leaving one with only a built-in singing in the ears. It also was reassuring to have a signal pistol in the backpack just in case they had problems spotting such a very small needle in such an outsize haystack when they returned in the evening to collect me.

Skuas Along Nansen's Beach – Franz Josef Land

Oil on board 18″ x 36″ (1993)

Those who love wilderness do so because it is just that. While they are not necessarily misanthropists, they are drawn to places where one may wander freely about, either alone or in chosen company, with little or no possibility of encountering another soul.

Somewhere in all this, however, there is a strange paradox. I can think of many places, islands mostly, that can be described as 'wilderness' by any definition, yet they have a link with mankind and spiritually, a very strong one. The link generally has to do with human courage and survival and leaves a discernible presence that calls for no great sensitivity to detect. Curiously enough, it is this human association that both enriches the place and makes it more of a wilderness at the same time. Such a place is Cape Norway on Franz Josef Land, high up in the Russian Arctic.

It was here that Nansen and Johannsen passed the winter of 1895–96 in a shelter made of stones and snow covered over with walrus skins nailed to a driftwood beam. They had travelled over 580 miles of the Arctic Ocean by sledge and canoe after leaving their ship *Fram* on her attempt to drift across the North Pole. They had hunted for food and oil for heat and light to carry them through the almost perpetual darkness. In the spring they emerged fit and well and pressed on home!

Many more polar bears than people will have walked that beach in the century that followed. The nail-scarred beam still lies across the depression in the stones, tiny fragments of leather still nestle in the crevices and there comes a sudden feeling of closeness to one of the great names in polar exploration – Fridtjof Nansen.

Sentiment breeds a curiously human sort of involvement with a place, an involvement to which the long-tailed skuas, passing regularly down the beach, must be totally oblivious.

Polar Bears – Lancaster Sound, North-West Territories

Oil on board 24" x 36" (1992)

Polar Bears in Pack-ice, Spitzbergen

Oil on board 8" x 20" (1996)

In describing the tiger, I mentioned the shattering experience of suddenly meeting in the wild for the first time, an animal that has been familiar from the nursery. It was exactly the same with the polar bear.

More than any other animal, this was the one I wanted to see. The longing was partly the result of what I already knew of the ice bear's mysterious, peripatetic, polar lifestyle and partly because I would obviously have to be there to see one.

The great moment came in 1981, up in the Kane Basin between Ellesmere Island and northern Greenland. I saw two bears together, and I even noted their co-ordinates – 79° 219N, 71° 339W. Since then there have been many polar bears in my life, some of them close enough for justifiable concern. With each one my admiration and affection has grown, both as animal and as subject.

The Duke of Wellington said that time spent on reconnaisance was never wasted and that must surely also apply to time spent simply watching, hour after hour, for something one dearly wants to see. I have spent hours, amounting to days, gazing across the pack-ice, eyes glued to binoculars to the very threshold of double vision. But I would do it again – any day. The delight of spotting that authentic fleck of creamy movement, far out on a sea of pristine white (though often polar bear-shaped) ice forms, is worth days of fruitless watch-keeping. It is even worth the occasional jibe of a shipmate, that Shackleton has his eye only on the Captain's bottle of akvavit, for the first to sight a bear.

Over the years since that first experience I have seen them gliding over rock-strewn slopes with fluid grace, ambling on open tundra, rolling in the snow like children, playing with their cubs, swimming unperturbed beyond sight of land, grabbing a seal and hauling it lifeless on to the ice.

These sights have now been spread around the whole of the Arctic; but the ice I feel, is their right and hereditary backcloth – ice for the ice bear. In such matters I am an incurable romantic. It seriously tarnishes my image of the polar bear, to watch them turning over rubbish as they regularly do, on a municipal dump – no matter how far north of the Arctic Circle.

123

Bar-headed Geese and the Highest Peaks

Oil on board 24" x 36" (1993)

Though once widespread and plentiful, the world's bar-headed goose population is probably little more than five thousand pairs. It is a bird of great beauty and romance and its unusual head and neck markings give it a strikingly Asiatic look. But its most exciting feature has to be the great heights attained in its annual migrations.

Bar-headed geese breed in central Asia as far south as Ladakh and Tibet. In October their southward movement begins, taking them all the way down to the marshes, lakes and *jheels* of India from the Indus valley eastwards to Assam and Burma. Across their path stand the Himalayas.

This painting of their southward autumn journey, shows the greatest of all peaks, Nuptse, Lhotse and Everest over which they must regularly pass and often at heights of over 30,000 feet. By March they will be heading north again, by much the same route.

I have never seen this spectacle, only read about it. But I have had the good fortune to work in this actual place and felt the wonder of it in the high, thin air. I was carrying the tripod for very special friends, Franz and Lydia Lazi, film-makers from Stuttgart with whom I have passed some wonderful times in some of the most improbable places on earth. My only contribution to their films is to write the commentaries for the end product. Carrying the tripod is my own way of making myself feel useful. It can also convince a charitable onlooker that I know something about photography.

The film that brought us here to the Khumbu Valley, was called *Delhi to Everest*, a profile of India and Nepal. When I had parked my tripod and Franz was busy filming from it, and Lydia was happy with her still-camera around the Thyangboche Monastery, I was free to draw. At the time however, I had no inkling of where and how the sketches might find a use. Finding references for the geese was a much easier matter – there they were waiting for me at the Wildfowl and Wetlands Trust, at Slimbridge.

Sandwich Terns on Number 3

Oil on board 18″ x 24″ (1994)

There comes a magic day each year, in late March, when a lively capping of white can be seen on one of the red marker buoys in the Kingsbridge Estuary. The sandwich terns are back – on Number 3.

Why always Number 3 is anybody's guess. The buoys are identical and there are four to choose from, but Number 3 is always the undisputed favourite. If a boat passes close to keep in the deep water channel, they will generally sit tight, reluctant to give way, and afford a fine view.

If one or two faint hearts *do* take wing, they will drift on to Number 2 or back to Number 4, but return as soon as the boat has passed. Number 3 will be consolidated once more with its full complement as they settle down, shoulders hunched and facing into the breeze.

These birds are the real harbingers of spring. Having worked their way north from West Africa, sometimes from as far as Angola, they are in full summer plumage when they arrive and their harsh call announces the event. The sight and sound of them proclaims that winter is over.

Number 3 buoy and its free-flying attendants present the kind of subject I find riveting. Again, it is contrasts that make it so. A man-made iron artefact, circular in section with straight and parallel sides, is as far removed from the free flowing lines of a tern as anything could be. To add to that, it is pillar-box red, actually *intended* to catch the eye, be easily noted and by very definition and purpose, totally out of harmony with anything natural. With the final touch of the robustly painted number, it completes a paradox where a note of discord becomes the essence of its appeal.

The very first time I saw it and even before my binoculars were lowered, I knew it had to become a picture. It did. And every year since, in the spring, when the terns are back again on Number 3, I watch them with the same joy, reap a little satisfaction from having 'had a go', but equally sure that one day I will succomb to the temptation to look again at the theme and try to find a different angle on such a compelling subject. If all else fails, I could always plan for a similar gathering on Number 2.

Successful Osprey

Oil on board 24" x 36" (1994)

The actions of predators about their business arouses a whole litany of convoluted and contradictory reactions. Some admire them with an almost sycophantic worship. Between this and the opposite extreme of unbridled hatred, comes every nuance of fascination, scientific interest and the kind of simple voyeurism generally associated with street accidents.

A sparrowhawk snatches a greenfinch off our nut basket and the debate comes up again about the thoughtlessness of providing packed lunches for raptors. Accusations of deliberately enticing passerines to their death, sounds a little harsh when levelled at someone with a heart as big as a house and reverence for all wild creatures.

What does it matter I ask, if the hawk takes its greenfinch off my bird-table or up in the back of the wood. It only needs one greenfinch. It is a predator – they never eat seeds, breadcrumbs, peanuts or even chocolate. They eat birds. and if they can catch no birds, they and their young, will die.

Even the homely blackbird, bouncing across the lawn to haul out a tightly stretched worm, comes in for some flak. Of course one has to admit that the nicest human beings are those that spare a thought for victims! I have seen people beside themselves with nail-biting anticipation at the dash and agility of a cheetah at full stretch, only to shed a Kleenex-full of tears for the gazelle. Yet, one feels happier that people *can* show such compassion. These are wholesome reactions by any human standards, but they lead to some curious attitudes and practices in the field of wildlife art.

No publisher will reproduce a picture that shows a dead anything, or even a hunted something. Active predation is out. It will not *sell*, they say, at least not on a popular level. This can even apply to a scene that could be construed as unfriendly. I was once told by a Christmas card buyer that a robin with its bill open was not acceptable. The open bill, apparently, suggested aggression (not song, as the artist may have intended) and aggression was taboo in a season of goodwill to all men (and robins).

Yet for some strange reason, the demise of a fish at the hands of a hunter, falls in a different category. No protestors mount campaigns in fishing ports, against brutality to haddock and there can be something close to a cheer of congratulation among watchers in a hide, when an osprey rises from a loch with a flapping fish.

What has to be said is that predators are designed to predate. For them a kill is the culmination of their entire purpose. Artistically, whatever the squeamish may feel, these creatures are displaying a moment in their behaviour pattern, that states what they are all about and as subjects they are at their best in the moment of achievement. They are presenting a fleeting glimpse of their nature that can be irresistible to even the most fish-friendly painter.

Little Egrets up South Pool Creek

Oil on board 24" x 18" (1995)
RSPB Fine Art Award 1995

As a bird, the little egret gets into my affections with a flying start. To begin with, it is elegant and very stylish while retaining as much versatility of shape as dough in the hands of a pastry cook. There are moments when its long legs and outstretched neck make it seem an endless and undernourished creature. When it subsides into rest it becomes almost spherical, with the short spike of a bill protruding at a tangent, presenting an effect that could be easily emulated by sticking a nail into an ice lolly. It is a bit of a comic. It is a gregarious bird but seems to be in agreeable harmony with its neighbours.

All its attitudes are immensely drawable and sometimes are even held long enough to make 'drawing' the accurate word rather than a 'field sketch', executed in extreme haste and with extreme economy of line. Then, in addition to all this aesthetic bounty, the bird is white and many will agree that white birds, like white flowers are the most beautiful. They are as pure and unsullied as a new canvas.

Art people will tell you that white is not a colour, any more than black is, and I suppose that in theory this is true. But it does not explain why I am so often asked how you would mix the 'colour' of a shadow falling on a white object, why white clouds are anything but white or why 'white' egrets when attempting to interpret them in paint, will call for every colour on the palette in the hope of rendering their 'whiteness' in a picture.

There have been a lot of chances to practise this. At the time we were planning to leave Chichester Habour and move to Devon, egrets were already increasing in numbers. They could always be seen from the bedroom window, exploring the tidal creek for shrimps and resting in the oaks that overhang it. As if old friends had moved with us we found a new and growing population already established on the Kingsbridge Estuary as well, doing just the same things.

A convenient study point I discovered early on, was the drain outlet below the town quay – just by the public loos. At low tide there they would be, mincing about with the occasional jab of a bill amongst loud and badly behaved gulls, looking like ladies dressed for Ascot forced to associate with shell suits, baseball caps and trainers.

Out in the Harbour, however, with the spring tide lapping under the lower branches of the oaks, they looked as if they had safely made it to the Royal Enclosure and were at last among their own kind. It was possible to lay the boat in close and watch them adorning their chosen tree with all their stately postural attributes and superb, white finery.

Every time I see them it is as if I had never seen one before, as if this subject in this sort of grouping had never been attempted. I would sail off home with the resolve to paint yet another picture featuring little egrets among the branches of a foreshore oak whose buds were swelling in the first warm days of March.

Inukshuk and Falcon – Cumberland Sound, Baffin Island

Oil on board 24″ x 18″ (1995)

'. . . acting like a human they have been there for generations. They attach us to our ancestors and to this land.'

Thus runs the Inuit explanation of an *Inukshuk*. They stand here and there in prominent places, providing quite apart from their primary intent, a very acceptable perch for a passing falcon. *Inukshuks* are like cairns – with more mystic implications.

This one stands close to the village of Pangnirtung on the western end of Baffin Island in Canada's North-West Territories, an area that enjoyed strong links with Yankee and Dundee whalers in the days of sail.

Local human history in so barren a wilderness has an immediate appeal and there is a little museum in the village to tell its story. I had already made a drawing of the *Inukshuk* when I came upon an Inuit poem so moving and redolent of the Esquimo culture, it reads like a verbal counterpart of the *Inukshuk* itself.

And there is only one great thing,
The only thing;
To live;
To see in huts and on journeys
The great day that dawns
And the light that fills the world.

133

Rockall with Fulmars

Oil on board 24″ x 36″ (1995)

To shipping forecast addicts 'Rockall' is a familiar name – a rectangular sea-area the size of Ireland, associated with the shallow Rockall Bank. Rockall itself though, is something uniquely special and so precise a location its co-ordinates must be stated in seconds – 57° 36′ 20″ N, 13° 41′ 32″W.

The solitary granite stack rises 70 feet from the ocean, 190 miles west of its nearest neighbour, St Kilda. In gale conditions seas will leap to twice its height, breaking clean over the summit. It is beyond doubt, the loneliest, wildest and for some, most evocative little piece of Britain and I have painted it with passing showers, in a south-westerly little more harsh than force 8, so that most of its shape can still be revealed.

By far the most regular visitors to Rockall are fulmars, attracted not by the lure of the lonely rock so much as the rich feeding in the shallow seas surrounding it. Shearwaters, gannets, storm petrels and other pelagic birds will pass, but fulmars, wheeling low over the waves on their stiff, silver wings are the trade-mark birds of Rockall, its parent bank and most of the North Atlantic as well.

A narrow ledge runs across the rock a few feet below the tip and from here the Union flag once flew from an improvised mast. Let into the rockface below is the more lasting bronze plaque of annexation, phrased in the traditional splendour of Crown and State upheld by the Royal Navy –

'By authority of Her Majesty Queen Elizabeth the Second, by the Grace of God of the United Kingdom of Great Britain and Northern Ireland and of her other realms and territories Queen, Head of the Commonwealth . . . a landing was effected this day upon this Island of Rockall from HMS *VIDAL*. The Union Flag was hoisted and possession of the Island was taken in the name of her Majesty.

R.H. Connell, Captain, HMS *VIDAL*, 18th September, 1955.'

VIDAL had circled the rock, fired a 21-gun salute and sailed away to Chatham. Gales in sea-area Rockall will long since have claimed the Union Flag – but the plaque remains steadfast and permanent, proclaiming, if only to passing fulmars, that this is an 'Isle' of our British Isles, the most westerly point of the United Kingdom.

Reproduced by courtesy of The Morrison Construction Group.

Pinkfeet – Kent Estuary

Oil on board 14" x 20" (1995)

My patron's request was to paint a picture of this very place because the location, in a way, took precedence over the birds. The birds, when the time came, were to be pink-footed geese.

Pinkfeet in the winter months, can be found in many parts of Britain. When I think of 'wild geese' in an abstract sense, it is always pinkfeet that fill the mental picture. Their inclusion therefore, at some later date, was the least problem and this is a happy way in which to set out on a painting assignment.

It had been years since I visited the Kent Estuary, in what was then Westmorland, and I found that several things had changed. But the racing tide over treacherous sands was the same and so was the eye-catching eminence of Whitbarrow, rising from the flat ground beyond, like some vast animal at rest.

There was much joy in painting this picture. It brought back memories of earlier visits here, but provided at the same time, the mental exercise of keeping an eye to the place the geese would take when the time came, in the finished composition.

It was with the geese in mind that the horizon came high in the picture, deepening the foreground of sea and sand. I wanted them to be flying low over this elemental No-Man's-Land as they so often do over areas they were designed for and where they feel secure and at home.

South Georgia

Oil on board 10″ x 16″ (1991)

The frontispiece of this book is a picture of South Georgia. It was painted for Dr John Levinson, then President of the Explorers Club, New York. It features Cumberland Bay with the Allardyce Range beyond and he had specified weather conditions so typical they endeared the place to him as much as to me.

An incredible island, South Georgia, wherein are gathered all the separate parts to make an encapsulation of the Southern Ocean and Antarctica combined (the mountains, glaciers, snow-fields, weather, wildlife) and a hugely disproportionate slice of all the human history. To me it can be an awesome place but it is also the most visually beautiful and paint-able island I have ever set foot upon.

This adjoining picture, only about 10″ x 16″, shows a more friendly aspect – the view across King Edward Cove towards Mt Sugartop and in the foreground, the memorial cross to Shackleton. This too was painted for a devotee, a young Army Captain stationed for a few weeks with his men, in the token garrison following the Falklands conflict. He too was there long enough to fall in love with it, not just for the island itself, but for the aura of human achievement that clings to it like a physical presence . . .

Triptych: South Georgia Landfall – the Arrival of the *James Caird*

Oil on boards 36" x 18", 36" x 49", 36" x 18"
(1996)

Stirring tales of survival at sea have been told by the thousand and by the nature of such happenings, all are different and comparison does not come easily. Two great epics, however, are similar enough in essence to be bracketed together and are often compared. One of them I have mentioned earlier – the voyage of William Bligh that followed the mutiny on the *Bounty*. The other also involves a ship's boat and of almost identical size – the 22-foot whaler *James Caird* and the Antarctic explorer, Sir Ernest Shackleton. Bligh's adversaries were tropical heat, thirst, hunger and cannibals. Shackleton's problems included thirst too, but also miserable cold, anxiety for others and the worst of the Southern Ocean in winter.

This triptych, the only one I have ever painted, was the brain-child of Peter and Carol Holland and the configuration of their room demanded it be painted in three separate components, set a few inches apart. It was to convey the skill and courage of men against odds that seemed insuperable. It is a concept of elements at their most fearsome – and in the middle of it all, a very small boat.

The story behind it begins in late November 1915, when Shackleton's expedition ship *Endurance* sank through the ice of the Weddell Sea. She had been beset since January, crushed and finally abandoned. There were now 28 men, a handful of dogs, stores and three ship's boats stranded on the ice and going where the drift took them – towards the north.

By 9 April 1916, the ice was being broken under them by a heavy swell. With open water ahead, they launched the boats. Six days later they had reached Elephant Island in the South Shetlands.

It must be remembered that the outside world had received no news of them since *Endurance* left Plymouth in August of 1914. Nobody knew their plight and no search vessel was expected, least of all at Elephant Island.

Shackleton's decision it could be said, made itself. He would prepare one sturdy boat by cannibalising the others, build up her sides a little, rig a mizen mast and attempt to deck her in with spars and spare sails. He picked his crew with wisdom – Worsley (Master of *Endurance*) Crean, McNeish, McCarty and Vincent, though all 28 had volunteered.

Nor did it take him long to decide that South Georgia must be his goal. It was further than other possibilities, but an altogether more feasible course, prevailing winds favoured him and he could lay the island in one long reach, with eased sheets and reasonable speed. He also knew that the whaling stations were manned year round and that there would be help for his 22 shipmates left under the command of Frank Wild, at the point on Elephant Island that now bears his name.

On 24 April *James Caird* set sail. The 800-mile voyage was horrendous. Everyone aboard knew full well that to have missed South Georgia, a relative speck and easily done in such weather, would have spelled a miserable end in the fastness of the Atlantic and the end too, for Wild and his men.

It takes some imagination to place oneself aboard *James Caird* under those conditions. Worsley, braced against the swaying mast, trying to hold his sextant on a sun that if there at all, was at best, a fuzz of light over a horizon more like the hills of Skye. His tables were soaked and shredding in his frozen fingers.

But on 8 May, two weeks later, out of the gloom ahead there suddenly appeared the mountains their eyes were straining to find and despite the exultation, the sight of an inhospitable leeshore that is any sailor's nightmare.

They stood off the coast for another two days desperately looking for a chance and it was a moment in this anxious time frame that suggested itself for my picture. The Fanning Ridge is the dominant feature with Mt Spaaman beyond and to the right, Newark Bay. I imagined the Lansing Glacier filling the bay as it must have done at the time – today it is much receded. *James Caird* took her chance and beached in King Haakon Bay some dis-

tance to the left on 10 May 1916.

Leaving their exhausted companions, Shackleton, Worsley and Crean set out some days later to cross the mountains – another story in itself. It had never before been attempted. With only a carpenter's adze and a coil of rope, they reached Stromness Whaling Station in about 30 hours. On 22 May, Worsley, with the station's help, recovered Vincent, McNeish and McCarty from their

camp at King Haakon Bay.

After a host of failed attempts to get through the ice, Shackleton and Worsley aboard the Chilean tug *Yelcho*, out of Punta Arenas, finally made it through to Elephant Island and on 30 August 1916 embarked Wild and all his men. Not a soul had been lost.

141

Water Worship – the Summary of a Lifelong Spell

It felt like an age spent in nail-biting impatience. The tide, depending on the gradient of the beach, seemed to move 'like the hands of a clock.' Finally the first ripples laid themselves at the watergate, demolished the little rampart of sand and in an instant the sea had filled the moat, to squeals of delight. In moments the sand-castle would topple and dissolve. An ephemeral little work of art, fashioned through hours of loving care and creative delight, had become a ritual sacrifice to the sea.

Sand-castle days pass on down the generations, losing nothing of their intrinsic joy. Then they emerge again, not just through sharing with children and grandchildren, but with even greater fervour into what becomes one's own second childhood.

My personal sand-castle period progressed swiftly into ponds – any sort of pond, no matter how small, that would hold water and thus animals and plants. I was happy to dig them out by the sweat of my brow and as effective liners had yet to be invented, try to consolidate them with cement. I suspect the satisfaction lay mainly in the making; they were seldom, for a variety of reasons, crowned with lasting success. It is doubtful if a single one will survive to confuse some passing archaeologist.

Then a new era dawned – and persists to this day. I discovered dams! From that moment on I could not look at even the humblest ditch, provided its water was on the move, without fantasising about its potential. My weasel eyes would scan the topography, visualising levels and the extent of what might be achieved in terms of ponds, lakes, swamps, inland seas!

My greatest, but alas short-lived, damming triumph occurred on my 13th birthday. We had a neighbour in those days, a farmer who enjoyed the unlikely though not inappropriate name of Bullet. On Mr Bullet's land, about half a mile from our house, there were two flattish fields (12 acres perhaps) separated by a sheep fence but more important, a drainage ditch which cut through a deep and narrow gully at the lower end. Inspiration struck in the proverbial 'blinding flash.' With the minimum of materials I could totally block this gully and boy-oh-boy we would be in business!

I confided in my elder brother, Allen. I needed his help and his far greater expertise in matters of contours, levels and industrial-scale hydrostatics in general. He was 14½. By dusk that day our dam was in place and the ditch already filling back.

It had rained heavily in the night to add to the fun but the spectacle that greeted the dawn outstripped all expectations. The scene from our bedroom window was pure Norfolk Broads. In the middle of it all the iron seat of Mr Bullet's horse-drawn field rake rose incongruously like Excalibur from the lake. The fence was entirely submerged and the seal of success provided by a flock of opportunist wigeon, overnight arrivals now contentedly up-ending in the shallows. Then we saw the dreaded Bullet himself. He was standing above the gully, cap pulled down and hands on hips, peering first at the dam, then across the water to our house. Even at that distance one could visualise the thought-balloon that rose from his head. He turned and walked purposely to his house. A minute or two later the telephone rang. My father answered it . . .

Water in its every form, salt and fresh, running and still, calm and gale-swept, from endless ice to geothermal steam has been my guiding element and provided for me the richest moments of visual and practical joy. Happily this continues and I am surprised I have not acquired webbed feet through some process of emotional evolution.

For the past eight years my wife and I have lived on the side of a Devon valley cradling a rock-strewn, fast-flowing river – water everywhere and all gravity driven. Springs from arcane underground systems break out on the hillside, supply the house in passing and run on down to the valley floor. Dams, of course, have had to happen at several levels, holding deep, clear pools and guiding their overflow onward. At the very bottom, on the riverside water-meadows is the home-made mere itself and it is as big as the one we had offered Mr Bullet all those years ago.

The thump and clatter of the JCB and the initial scars have long since gone. Fortuitous deposits of clay hold its water and the lively springs restore the evaporation of summer. Vegetation, planted and self-sown, has transformed the margins into inviting green jungles where the crake of moorhens sounds from deep seclusion.

Mr Bullet in person had been our dambuster, denying us the thrill of pulling the biggest bath-plug one could imagine. But fulfilment at last is here in the permanence of my present and entirely legitimate creation. Moreover I have learned that when it comes to 'art' in its broadest interpretation, a spade is as satisfying a tool as a paintbrush as well as a fearsome competitor.

The birds seem to appreciate this, as do the frogs, toads, newts and grass snakes. Mallard and teal drop in at dusk, Canada geese stop by, the sentinel heron and the odd egret up from the estuary five miles downstream. Swallows, swifts and martins skim the surface and a furtive snipe probes the sedges. Most spectacular of all, when the big dragonflies are hatching in high summer, a hobby will arrive, dropping out of the sun like the Red Baron, streaking across the mere with the speed of an arrow, to snap them out of the air.

The sheer magnetism of water for so many life forms proclaims its magic. It is almost a 'religion' and one with an infinite following. I can see that this is set to be what is now referred to as an 'on-going situation'; and on it will assuredly go until the onset of decreptitude renders navvying impossible or I absent-mindedly sever a foot with a chainsaw.

Recently I read a statistic claiming that the two longest-lived professions were artists and country parsons. It had to do with factors like clean air and lack of 'stress'. It was also unkind enough to mention a lifestyle that makes few physical demands. At all events I am prepared to accept it. But what it failed to mention is that the greatest bonus of all to painters – more so even than the clergy – is that 'retirement' as such, does not appear in their vocabulary.

Woodley Wood Farm – A Buzzard's View

Oil on board 18" x 24" (1994)